"He has showed you, O man, what is good; and what does the Lord require of you but to do justice, and to love kindness, and to walk humbly with your God?"—Micah 6:8

"But if any one has the world's goods and sees his brother in need, yet closes his heart against him, how does God's love abide in him? Little children, let us not love in word or speech but in deed and in truth."—1 John 3:17-18

"In Germany they came first for the Communists, and I didn't speak up because I wasn't a Communist. Then they came for the Jews, and I didn't speak up because I wasn't a Jew. Then they came for the trade unionists, and I didn't speak up because I wasn't a trade unionist. Then they came for the Catholics, and I didn't speak up because I was a Protestant. Then they came for me, and by that time no one was left to speak up."—Pastor Martin Niemoeller

POLITICS:

A Case for Christian Action

Robert D. Linder &
Richard V. Pierard

InterVarsity Press
Downers Grove
Illinois 60515

*Second printing
March 1975*

*InterVarsity Press is the
book publishing division of
Inter-Varsity Christian
Fellowship, a student movement
active on campus at hundreds of
universities, colleges and schools
of nursing. For information about
Inter-Varsity Christian
Fellowship, write IVCF, 233
Langdon, Madison WI 53703.*

*ISBN 0-87784-356-2
Library of Congress Catalog
Card Number: 73-77850*

*Printed in the United
States of America*

This book is dedicated to our students

Contents

Preface

A number of influences lay behind our decision to undertake this project: growing to maturity in poor to moderate circumstances; conversion to Christ in the teen years; commitment to biblical authority; an expanding awareness of the social implications of the Christian gospel; the impact on our lives of the works of such men as Edward J. Carnell, Kenneth Scott Latourette, Herbert Butterfield, C. S. Lewis and Eric Maria Remarque; exposure to the rigors and discipline of graduate training in history; the challenge of teaching in the dynamic atmosphere of today's university; the opportunity to work closely with the present generation of students; our personal political involvement and experiences; and an increasing concern for the future of our children and the world they will someday inherit.

We know there are both difficulties and risks involved in writing a book on Christianity and politics in this day and age. One difficulty is that on these two subjects almost everybody imagines he is an expert, and so virtually anything said about them is bound to offend some individual or group. In other words, what we have to say is bound to be controversial. Furthermore, some will raise the question of whether another book on the topic is justified or needed, since there seem to be so many other volumes on politics and religion and since many other sources of political information and awareness are available to the general public, namely, radio, TV and newspapers. Moreover, what we write today on this volatile and rapidly changing subject may be out of date tomorrow. Finally, a brief treatise runs the risk that many of our fellow believers will consider it to be poor Christianity and not a few of our fellow academicians will regard it as a dissipation of scholarly energies.

Yet it seems to us that facing all of the difficulties and risks involved is worthwhile if we succeed in motivating Christian students to examine—or perhaps re-examine—their views on the relationship between their faith in Christ and the world of political involvement. And we think Christians of other age groups will find this volume helpful as well. Undoubtedly, our readers will not agree with everything we have to say, but we hope that our work will supply useful ideas and guidelines for Christian students as they attempt to come to grips with the great political and social issues of our time. In any case, our aim is to provoke discussion and not dissension, reflection and not recrimination, political awareness and not political antagonism. We would, in fact, encourage readers to follow up this volume by reading some of the books listed on pages 147-55.

We want to emphasize that this is not an "issues" book; the questions we deal with are illustrative, provocative and currently in the public eye.[1] Further, we recognize that a movement is afoot in the land which stresses "people-centered politics," and we want to make clear that we are very much in sympathy with this development. Therefore, if this discussion seems to be somewhat of a polemic for a people-oriented approach to politics, that is because we have designed it that way.

We realize that today's young people do not possess some mysterious quality which makes them automatically superior to those who have gone before. But, as President Richard M. Nixon pointed out in his first inaugural address, today's youth are better educated and seem to be

". . . more committed, more passionately driven by conscience than any generation in our history."[2] We hope to influence them to play a larger role in current political life so that they will be prepared for the day in the near future when the mantle of leadership will fall upon their shoulders. Since we are committed to people-centered politics, some biases may emerge with which not all readers will concur. Feel free to discount these but try not to overlook our main message: Young Christians need to take a stand, speak out and get involved now.

This book owes much to many friends and critics over the years. To attempt to name them all would be pointless as well as unnecessary for they know who they are. Also, it goes without saying that each of our wives—Jean Ann Linder and Charlene Pierard—and all of our children reluctantly but graciously dispensed with our presence for many hours on Saturdays and holidays in order for us to have the time to research and produce this volume. We deeply appreciate their understanding and forbearance. We are thankful for the assistance of our wives and of Betty Bailey in typing the manuscript. Finally, we wish to thank the Christian students at Kansas State University and Indiana State University for providing the inspiration for writing this work. We believe in them and have great hope for the future because of the depth of commit-

ment to Christ and the quality of life we see in them.

Robert D. Linder
Department of History
Kansas State University

Richard V. Pierard
Department of History
Indiana State University

chapter one

Do Christianity
and Politics Mix?

A noted scholar recently made a study of evangelism and social concern, and as part of his research he sent out questionnaires to a number of evangelists inquiring about their attitudes toward involvement in social issues. One respondent who is engaged in student work on a university campus returned his questionnaire unanswered and appended the following comment: "Dear Mr. ____ : This is out of our field of calling. Wish we could help."[1]

Regeneration and a Cup of Cold Water/
This evangelist's attitude of indifference to or ignorance of social and political problems is

hardly an isolated phenomenon. Every Christian active in any form of public life has heard it expressed again and again, in a hundred different ways. However, there is no real biblical basis for such a view, and many prominent Christian leaders have tried to pound home this fact. David Moberg has pointed out that religion is never "purely personal." It is not limited to communication with God alone but always involves social relationships with men.[2] Twenty years ago, in a famous passage in *Peace with God,* Billy Graham unequivocally insisted: "Jesus taught that we are to take regeneration in one hand and a cup of cold water in the other. Christians, above all others, should be concerned with social problems and social injustices."[3] This was reaffirmed in the 1966 Wheaton Declaration on the Church's Worldwide Mission, which plainly stated: "We will demonstrate anew God's concern for social justice."[4]

J. N. D. Anderson, Professor of Oriental Laws in the University of London, has urged Christians to seek out careers in all areas of life so that through their vocations they might "influence public standards" and be the salt that seasons every facet of society.[5] *Decision* magazine editor Sherwood Wirt noted recently,

> *[In modern society] interdependence has supplanted independence as the rule of life. The evangelical's social conscience requires that he*

*play his part as a member of the team of hu-
manity. If there is poverty, he should be
taking a lead in seeking to eradicate it. If
there is injustice, he should be an Amos point-
ing it out. If there is corruption, he should be
helping to turn the rascals out. If there is
waste, he should be acting the role of good
steward.*[6]

In his address at Urbana 70 Myron S. Augsburger underscored the need for a revolution
that would bring Christian values to bear on today's society, elevate once again the value of
persons and tackle the basic problems of the
contemporary world.[7]

In other words, even though the primary responsibility of Christians is to believe and spread
the gospel, God has also commanded them to
serve him in their daily lives, including the realm
of politics. This is the thrust of the preceding
statements, and it will be abundantly demonstrated in the following chapters, which outline
the biblical basis for Christian political involvement. One of the most significant areas of Christian concern is politics, *the formation and implementation of public policy for the public good.*
Attention to the role of citizenship is obviously
an important aspect of politics in a democratic
system of government like that found in many
countries of the Western world. But simply to
discharge the elementary responsibilities of citi-

zenship, such as voting, paying taxes and obeying laws, *is insufficient* since it does not allow the Christian to fulfill his gospel obligations in the fullest sense in a modern democratic context. Rather, the Christian should plunge into practical political activity as deeply as his personality and talents will permit.[8]

The command to serve God in society has particular significance for the college generation, those between the ages of eighteen and twenty-five who are now crossing the threshold of maturity. These people hold in their hands the keys to the future and need to be challenged to take seriously the responsibilities of citizenship. Since the minimum voting age was recently dropped to eighteen in the United States and already has been or is about to be lowered in many of the other democracies, this volume may be equally helpful to those currently in high school who need to be made aware of their impending political obligations.

Many people are encouraged about the future because it seems to them that young people currently are more open to change than their elders and that there is great potential for good in the new generation of Christian believers. If this observation about the high quality of the character and faith of today's younger Christians is correct, then it is doubly important that they have an understanding of politics and the political processes, and that they become involved in democratic political and social action.

Some Key Words and Concepts/

Since this book is written mainly for the Christian student, some things in it may be incomprehensible to those who adhere to non-Christian religions or no religion at all. Further, we restrict our definition of the Christian faith to that of historic, orthodox Christianity; that is, the acceptance of (1) the Bible as the basis of religious authority, (2) the need for individual spiritual regeneration (salvation) through faith in Jesus Christ and (3) the lordship of Christ in all of life. Those who construe Christianity in such a manner are frequently referred to as "evangelicals," especially in the English-speaking countries. Many Christians have formulated elaborate creedal statements, but the above-mentioned points must of necessity comprise the foundation for those creeds if they are to stand in the historic Christian tradition.[9]

We deliberately avoid the term *church* in this work, not only because it is trite but even more because of the vagueness with which it is used in popular parlance. For instance, Ted Ward has shown that no less than four meanings of the word *church* are in common use among Christians today. Two of these are biblical usages, namely, the entire body of those who have trusted Christ throughout all ages and a specific group of believers assembled in some particular region, town or place. The other two, which originated in the course of Christian history and are clearly nonbiblical, are the church as a building and the church as a denomination or organized religious system. Thus, the term *church* can mean the people who belong to Christ either corporately or in small groups, a physical structure, or an ecclesiastical system.[10] Since innumerable books and articles currently spell out the political and social responsibility of the church,[11] we will direct our attention to Christian young people and their obligations both as individuals and as members of various groups which are committed to political and social action. An example of such a group could be a church or a political party or even an Inter-Varsity chapter.

Political involvement means active participation in the life of the state. As will be shown in the next chapter, the state is a divinely ordained institution, the primary function of which is to provide law, order, justice and the opportunity to pursue individual happiness for a geographically delineated segment of human society. Working from this base, we can postulate that the state was made for man and not man for the state. This is a fundamental tenet of modern democratic political theory and is in harmony with the teachings of historic Christianity. The government is responsible for conducting the affairs of the state. It functions on a number of different planes, from the subdistrict of a town to the national level, depending upon the size of a country and the nature of its political structure. Because of the pervasive influence of modern democratic ideals, in almost all states today the citizenry is allowed some measure of participation in the selection of personnel to serve in the government. A good regime is one in which laws provide a just and equitable social order for all citizens of the state.

Seizing the Opportunities and Filling the Voids/
Since the government is composed of human, not divine, beings—regardless of the assumptions of some current leaders to the contrary—it will be no better than the people who make it up. If Christians refuse to become politically involved, the state will be deprived of the services of a large body of citizens whose personal relationship with the Creator gives them a profound sense of concern for the needs of their fellow men. This is especially true in the Western democracies. Congressman John B. Anderson puts it well: "If Christians leave opportunities for participation open and unfilled, the void will be filled by those who do not necessarily share a similar ethical concern."[12]

Hence, Christian young people should avoid any type of other-worldly pietism or nihilistic frustration that leads to passivity and noninvolvement in political affairs. They should also look with apprehension upon those visionaries of the left—Christian or non-Christian—who call for a radical rejection of the existing political system in favor of some utopian, even anarchistic, new order. Both extremes are really sideline approaches. The Christian student has too much to contribute to the game to remain on the bench.

Since this book has been designed to help Christian students exercise the principles of their faith in the society in which they live—namely, the college or university campus—it is subject to certain inherent limitations. For example, we do not intend to tell the Jew or Muslim or agnostic how to apply his principles. We assume that those who adhere to Christianity will operate from a different conceptual framework and that their conclusions may or may not be in accord with those of other religious viewpoints. Nevertheless, we are convinced that applying Christian principles to the contemporary world will make it a better place for all people to live, and we encourage young Christians to devote themselves to this task. These principles are directly related to the question of political involvement itself, which is discussed in the next chapter.

chapter two

Why Should I Get Involved?

Should I be interested in politics? Oh, no, Lord, not me! My citizenship is in heaven. My job here on earth is to win souls. You placed me on the campus to proclaim the gospel to my fellow students, not to get involved in political manipulations. Besides, politicians are dirty, corrupt men who have no principles and will do anything to get a person's vote. Followers of Jesus Christ are to keep themselves unspotted by the world and to abstain from all appearance of evil. It's in your Word!

Is this just a caricature of evangelical thinking on political participation? Yes, to some extent, but how often have you said this yourself or heard other Christians in your student group or church congregation utter such statements? These are objections which every believer active in public life has had to confront and settle in his own mind. A strong case exists against Christians becoming involved in politics, and the concerned student must be prepared to meet these arguments head on with scriptural teaching and practical answers.

Objections to Christian Political Involvement/
One of the most common contentions is that *the world is evil* and Christians must refrain from contact with it as much as possible. They are not part of the world; Christ has removed them from it. A host of Bible verses can be marshaled to support this position. "You are not of the world, but I chose you out of the world, therefore the world hates you" (Jn. 15:19). "They are not of the world, even as I am not of the world" (Jn. 17:16). "My kingdom is not of this world" (Jn. 18:36, AV). "Our commonwealth [citizenship] is in heaven" (Phil. 3:20).

Further, believers are enjoined: "Do not love the world or the things in the world. If any one loves the world, love for the Father is not in him" (1 Jn. 2:15). Not only are Christians forbidden to live in conformity with the world (Rom. 12:2), but also the Bible warns that "whoever wishes to be a friend of the world makes himself an enemy of God" (Jas. 4:4). Since followers of Christ are commanded to avoid every form of evil and keep themselves unstained from the world, they must separate themselves from iniquity, darkness and uncleanness (1 Thess. 5:22; Jas. 1:27; 2 Cor. 6:14-17). Jesus gave his life to "deliver us from this present evil world, according to the will of our God and Father" (Gal. 1:4). No matter what Christians may do to try to improve conditions in the world, their labors will come to naught. "Evil men and imposters will go on from bad to worse" (2 Tim. 3:13) is the clear, unequivocal teaching of the Scripture.

A second line of argument is that the believer's sole responsibility and task is to *win men to Christ.* The wise man is the one who wins souls (Prov. 11:30). God has placed Christians as watchmen to warn the lost that they must flee from the wrath that is to come by turning from their wicked ways to Jesus Christ. He will hold Christians accountable at the judgment if they fail to proclaim the message of salvation (Ezek. 3:17-21; Mt. 3:7). Now is the day of salvation; God may not allow many of these souls any more time (2 Cor. 6:2). Believers must be about their Father's business: "Rescue the perishing, care for the dying, tell them of Jesus who is mighty to save."

The Christian message is "spiritual," not

"social." Christians have no time to help mend the fallen, corrupt society that comprises the world around them. Christ is coming soon and then the earth will be renewed. To spend precious time in political and social action aimed at patching up the world is futile. It is a Satanic delusion that tragically results in the condemnation of millions to a Christless eternity in hell, because it distracts Christians from the work their Lord has assigned them.

Passages referring to Jesus' concern for physical needs—such as his Sermon on the Mount (Mt. 5—7); his affirmation of compassion for the multitudes (Mt. 9:36); his declaration in the synagogue at Nazareth that he was sent to preach good news to the poor, imprisoned, blind and oppressed (Lk. 4:18); and his statement in the Olivet discourse that ministering to others would be accounted as ministering to him (Mt. 25:45)—do not imply that the responsibility to win souls is secondary. Further, these assertions must be understood spiritually, not literally, and some are binding only for those living in a different dispensation than ours. They "were for the Jews" or "will be for the kingdom" and are not applicable to our age.

A third argument concerns *individual piety*. The thrust of the First Commandment ("You shall have no other gods before me") suggests that nothing should take precedence over loving and serving the Lord. Christians must forsake family and possessions for Christ, seeking first the kingdom of God and his righteousness (Mt. 19:29; Mt. 6:33).

Christians, then, should not allow the temptation of political involvement to distract them from being concerned with their own spiritual condition. The prospect of Christ's imminent appearing is a particularly compelling reason for believers to purify themselves (1 Jn. 3:2-3). They should set their minds "on things that are above, not on things that are on earth" (Col. 3:2). Since they have died to sin and their life is hid with Christ, and hence at the second coming they will appear with the Savior in glory (Col. 3:2-4), redeemed individuals should live and walk by the Spirit of God; their life in this world should be "sober, upright, and godly" (Gal. 5:25; Tit. 2:12). The apostle Paul declared that "godliness is of value in every way," both for the present life and as preparation for the future one (1 Tim. 4:8). Believers should cleanse themselves "from every defilement of body and spirit, and make holiness perfect in the fear of God" (2 Cor. 7:1).

Fourth, because *God is in control,* his inscrutable providence in its own time will remedy injustice and oppression. He is the Sovereign of the universe and has made the world the way it is. Since God has also predetermined the future, he will work out everything in accordance with his good pleasure. Only through prayer can Christians bring about change and improvement in human conditions. They must never rely on the "arm of flesh" (2 Chron. 32:8; Jer. 17:5), since human effort will achieve absolutely nothing that is contradictory to the divine purpose. What God creates is good; man's handiwork invariably goes astray and falls short of the mark. Vernon C. Grounds has parodied the spirit of this kind of evangelical quietism in his paraphrase of a popular old hymn:

> *Sit down, O men of God:*
> *His kingdom He will bring*
> *Whenever it may please his will.*
> *You cannot do a thing!*[1]

Two other arguments against political involvement need to be mentioned. They are frequently voiced by the general public as well as by committed Christians. One is that *politics is dirty* and therefore should be avoided. At its worst, politics implies crookedness, shady deals, corruption, high-handed power plays and evil scheming in smoke-filled rooms. Why would any man of integrity want to enter politics? After all, is not an honest politician one who, when bought, stays bought? And there is the typical office seeker, caricatured in a *New Yorker* cartoon by Whitney Darrow, Jr., who declares to an audience of potential voters: "I have never stooped, my friends, nor will I now stoop, to the kind of vicious falsehoods, mud-slinging, and personal vilification indulged in by my opponent and his Commie pals."[2]

Even at its best, politics means compromise, and for Christians this is not permitted. Compromise is an evil thing to be avoided at all costs. Followers of Jesus Christ must be people of high moral principles, whose conduct is governed by absolute standards of right and wrong. The unethical behavior and unprincipled compromises which characterize political life are anathema to believers who are living according to the teachings of the Scriptures and walking in the Holy Spirit.

The second view frequently expressed is that *political involvement does not make any difference anyway.* This is the stance of political apathy. It may take the form of a conscious decision to drop out—a common practice by many disillusioned former adherents to the New Left—or it may mean turning one's back on the world's problems and concentrating on earning money and raising a family in a quiet corner of suburbia—the typical middle-class approach. Who really cares what the little man thinks?—all the decisions are made by the party bosses. There is no difference between parties and candidates; they are like "Tweedledum and Tweedledee." Their platforms and policies are vague and ambiguous, while the candidates are trying to be all things to all men.

The Christian twist to this argument is that Jesus said: "My kingship is not of this world" (Jn. 18:36). Since the Lord and his disciples never involved themselves in political affairs, Christians are not obligated to do so either. Because the message of the gospel is "spiritual," believers should devote their efforts to religious causes. They can do nothing about the current political situation, and, if they could, what real difference would it make? The truly significant battles are fought in the spiritual, not the political, arena. Worldlings think they can accomplish something practical and maybe even improve the moral tone of society. Real children of God know otherwise and do not waste their time in fruitless political activity.

The Objections Answered/
These reasons for noninvolvement have a persuasive ring to them, but they are inadequate rationalizations and must be recognized as such. If concerned Christian students probe more deeply into the problem, they will soon see the shallowness of this sort of head-in-the-sand religion. Before they are thoughtlessly accepted any further, these six common arguments against Christian participation in politics need to be examined

more closely in the light of God's Word, history and political reality.

The world may be tainted by sin, but it still belongs to God. It is his by right of creation and is under his dominion and providence. In fact, he so deeply loved the world that he gave his only begotten Son to die for it (Jn.3:16), and he has commanded Christians to bear witness to the divine love in all parts of the earth (Acts 1:8). Certainly this must include testifying that the love of Christ is the answer to the world's complexities. Mennonite historian Alan Kreider accurately notes that "the practical manifestations of the Spirit of Christ—complete brotherhood, genuine mutual love and concern, selflessness—should serve as a sign or parable to an unbelieving generation."[3]

Further, Christians have been placed in the world to minister to it. Why are believers not immediately brought into the presence of Christ in heaven at the time of their conversion? The sovereign God could do this if he wished, but he does not. Instead the redeemed are left in the world to serve as salt and lights (Mt. 5:13-16). Through their witness and actions they, like salt, preserve the world from the decay which is the result of evil. As lights, they guide those people living in the darkness and night of sin to Jesus Christ, the light of the world. They are expected to give themselves in ministry to others—feed them, quench their thirst, clothe and shelter them, comfort them in loneliness and despair (Mt. 25:31-45). The "salt-light principle" will of necessity draw Christians into political action because nowadays only governments and a few large cooperative agencies possess the measure of wealth and power that can provide for the needs of the less-favored in society. Individual persons simply lack the resources to do this by themselves.

Nowhere does Scripture indicate that God approves of the excesses and evils of wicked rulers. Should Christians not work to change or replace a regime that neglects basic human needs? It seems impossible to escape the logic of the argument that if we love our neighbors as ourselves, we will do what we can to improve their lives. This definitely will involve more than taking up an extra collection for the needy on Sunday morning or depositing a Christmas basket on the doorstep of some poor family. Sir Frederick Catherwood, an evangelical layman and former Director General of the National Economic Development Office of Great Britain, correctly suggests that a refusal to become involved in public affairs is a breach of the second great commandment (Mk. 12:31). According to Catherwood, "To try to improve society is not worldliness but love. To wash your hands of society is not love but worldliness."[4]

This leads naturally to the second argument, the responsibility to direct men to Christ. All too often this is a red herring thrown out by those who wish to remain aloof from the problems of the world. The sacred-secular antithesis so popular among conservative Christians has no foundation in the Word of God. Jesus himself healed bodies as well as souls, changed water into wine, fed multitudes of hungry people and raised a widow's son from the dead. Just because spiritual things should take first place in our lives does not mean that nothing else matters.

Servants of Christ are obligated to minister to the whole man, meeting both his spiritual *and* material needs. On a number of occasions Jesus reproved the Pharisees, the "fundamentalists" of his day, for their shortcomings in this regard. They scrupulously observed the fine points of the law, offered up long prayers, tithed faithfully and acted piously in the presence of others, but at the same time were callously indifferent to the needs of their fellowmen. Christ violated the ceremonial rules regarding the Sabbath by allowing his hungry disciples to pick grain to eat and by healing a man with a withered hand and another one with dropsy; this indicates clearly the high value he placed on human concerns (Mt. 12:1-13; Lk. 14:1-4). The disciple who gives a cup of cold water to a needy person will not go unrewarded (Mt. 10:42). In the story of the good Samaritan, which poignantly illustrates genuine neighbor-love, Jesus singled out for commendation the despised and apostate foreigner who physically aided the injured man, not the spiritual leaders of the Jewish nation (Lk. 10:29-37). If Christians love their neighbors as themselves, they cannot and will not place politics and religion in two different spheres.

With respect to the third argument, if Christians devote all their time to "spiritual" activities and cultivating personal piety, they will undoubtedly neglect other tasks of a more mundane nature which God clearly has in mind for them. These include exercising stewardship over God's creation and carrying on the ministry of reconciliation. Christians are to care for God's physical world, making good use of the resources of nature. Francis Schaeffer remarks that God treated his creation with integrity, bestowing value upon each thing. If believers wish to be in the right relationship with God, they should treat these divinely created things in the same way God himself does.[5]

In like manner they should be working to reconcile men with their neighbors. As ambassadors of Christ the people of God should be laboring in the world to heal the alienation of individuals, classes, nations and races (2 Cor. 5:18-20). The late Jaymes P. Morgan of Fuller Theological Seminary properly concluded:

The Scriptures entrust those who control the life of society with a responsibility for creating and preserving the best society that it is within fallen man's power to create and sustain. And the price of living in a nation where government is "by the people," where the control of national life is invested in the hands of the common man, is that there is no place to hide from the eyes of God on that day when he shall look for those who are responsible.[6]

Should Christians retire to the sidelines and quietly wait for divine intervention, as the fourth objection suggests? One will search the Scriptures in vain to find support for such passivity. Who shall enter the kingdom of heaven? Jesus answers: not the man who piously mouths "Lord, Lord" but he who *does* the will of the Father (Mt. 7:21). This activist emphasis characterizes the whole scope of the Christian life. Peter admonished God's people to *do right,* by this action silencing those who reject the gospel message (1 Pet. 2:15). Paul said to the Galatian churches: "Let us do good to all men" (Gal. 6:10). James specifies that believers must be "doers of the word" and not passive hearers only, and he spells out in detail what doing right involves. Christians must care for orphans and widows, show no partiality for the wealthy and feed those who are hungry. "So faith by itself, if it has no works is dead" (Jas. 1:22, 27; 2:17, 26).

A corollary is that Christians must be *taught* how to do good. One of the most popular evangelical misconceptions is that conversion automatically changes a man's basic attitude toward his fellows. Racist practices by many evangelical church members in the United States or the uncompromising stances of many professing Christians in Northern Ireland give the lie to this myth. An unnamed missionary to South Africa, writing in *HIS* magazine, graphically observed that "all too often people are only converted to the Jesus who saves their souls. They never know the Jesus who preached the Sermon on the Mount. . . . The missionary who tries to remain uninvolved in life on any level other than the spiritual will produce converts who uphold the status quo."[7] Thus, the words of the psalmist should be on the lips of every servant of Christ: "Teach me thy way, O Lord" (Ps. 27:11).

The argument that Christians should have nothing to do with politics because it is a dirty business smacks of irresponsibility and is open to criticism from several quarters. Senator Mark O. Hatfield notes that the decision of good, honest people to avoid politics "creates a serious vacuum of morality in places of public leadership." Christians have stood by as neutral observers while the contest between good and evil has been fought in the political arena. Good men often have done nothing and consequently have allowed the ungodly to win the battle by default. As this Christian legislator eloquently affirms,

> *For the Christian man to reason that God does not want him in politics because there are too many evil men in government is as insensitive as for a Christian doctor to turn his back on an epidemic because there are too many germs there. For the Christian to say that he will not enter politics because he might lose his faith is the same as for the physician to say that he will not heal men because he might catch their diseases.*[8]

Politics itself is not inherently evil or good—the term refers merely to the conduct of public affairs. It degenerates into a dirty business only because people allow it to do so. The way the game of politics is played largely reflects the kind of individuals who are in the game. Obviously, if the political system is left to those who play dirty, it will be dirty. On the other hand, if enough decent and honorable people become involved in political activity, politics will be clean and honest. Were a significant number of Christians to enter political life, their impact on public morality could be impressive.

Even as things stand today, Daniel Grant, a political scientist and widely known Southern

Baptist lay leader, questions the validity of the "dirty politics" notion and labels it a puzzling but persistent myth. No one ever asserts that democracy is dirty, although politics is the process by which people govern themselves in a democracy. The dirty politics mentality results in a bizarre system where we treat our politicians as unsavory characters at the same time that we charge them with preserving our civilization. Also, we hear much about dirty politics but seldom anything about "dirty business" or "dirty education."[9]

Grant offers two reasons for this confused public image of politics. For one thing, the work of politicians is conducted in the full glare of public scrutiny—the news media and politicians out of office never take their eyes off those who are in power. At the same time business firms, banks, labor unions, college faculties and church deacon boards operate in relative secrecy. A city council meeting or a state legislature session is usually open to all—something that seldom is the case with these other segments of society.

Moreover, Americans in particular have a double standard of morality for persons in and out of politics. Behavior which is taken for granted in other areas of life is condemned in government officials. For instance, the son of a business executive can be brought into the firm and pushed toward the top. If, however, a public official did this for his son, his action would be regarded as "nepotism," not as an understandable expression of family loyalty. When a businessman receives a fur coat from a supplier, it is considered an accepted business practice, justified as "developing good will." A similar gift to a government purchasing agent would be labeled a "bribe" or "graft." Political scientist Grant rightly insists:

> *The burden of proof is on the one who thinks that the politics of running government is any more dirty or dishonest than the politics of running a bank, labor union, trucking company, college, or even a church. Because of its life in a goldfish bowl, the governmental process may actually be a bit cleaner and more honest than the process of running most other social institutions.*[10]

Politics is also distasteful to many Christians because of its emphasis upon the acquisition and use of power, and the role of compromise in the political process. However, the exercise of political power is the essence of self-government, and without power no political program could ever be put into effect. Compromise, with its emphasis upon give-and-take, is the primary method of accomplishing desired ends in the political realm, especially in a democracy. The opposite of compromise is despotic, arbitrary tyranny. Power and compromise are fundamental aspects of political behavior and, like politics itself, are not intrinsically good or bad.

Conflict lies at the heart of politics, a fact incomprehensible to the idealist who, moved by a sense of moral urgency, invariably sees the world in *either-or* terms. Politics is a never-ending search for a foundation that will support the mass of contradictions that make up modern society. Political activity that seeks to implement inflexible principles or "fundamental truth" very often leads to tyranny. Sociologist Ralf Dahrendorf points out the significance of ongoing struggle for political power: "Competition keeps societies open to change and prevents the dogmatization of error. Aversion to conflict is a basic trait of authoritarian political thought, which means in effect that the government loses control of change, and the citizens lose their freedom."[11]

The apathetic "it makes no difference anyway" outlook is as irresponsible as the dirty politics rationalization (if not more so). Of all people, Christians should be the ones to reject this view. If the whole of society lies within the purview of God's care and providence, and he uses human beings to carry out his purposes, then Christians should be active participants in the maintenance of an orderly world. As evangelical author A. N. Triton aptly remarks, "If God cares for good laws, how can we fail to be active in getting His will done on earth?" After all, good laws and customs do matter since they make it possible for everyone to live a more fully human life and thus help fulfill God's creative intention for mankind.[12]

One of the great cop-outs of our time is the suggestion that because Christ's kingdom is not of this world, his followers should stay out of political life. To be sure, Jesus and his disciples never belonged to a political party, sought positions in the government, made political speeches or advanced a specific action program. But neither did any of them practice medicine or law, join a labor union, serve in the army or operate a store, and yet Christians today do all of these. For a believer to neglect his political responsibilities represents not only poor citizenship but also a faulty understanding of his role in the present world. As will be shown later, in many instances a Christian's actions in the political realm have been decisive. Participation in public life really does make a difference and Christian students should not overlook the potentialities of this area of service.

The Christian and the State/

Young people today are bombarded with negative expressions about government. These are particularly prevalent in their church and among their peers. Yet the Scriptures clearly teach that the *institution* of human government is divinely ordained and that Christians are to obey and submit to the state (Rom. 13:1-2). Why was government established? What are its functions? What is the believer's obligation to the governing authorities?

Why was government instituted? For one thing, man was made a creature of community. In the Garden of Eden God decreed: "It is not good that man should be alone" (Gen. 2:18). And Paul reaffirmed this principle in Romans 14:7: "None of us lives to himself, and none of us dies to himself." No man can live at the level of pure individualism; from the moment of his birth to his final repose in death, a man requires the assistance and involvement of others in every aspect of his life. Each person depends upon the creativity and labor of others for his food, clothing, housing, education, health care, cultural enjoyment and spiritual guidance. As a social being, man needs government to enable him to live in harmony with his fellows. "While men are alike in needing human association," says Foy Valentine, "they differ in ability and self-control so that government is an absolute necessity in providing some minimum rules for their relationships with, and responsibilities to, one another."[13]

Another reason for the institution of government is human sinfulness. Man's original act of disobedience in the Garden of Eden transformed him into a sinful, corrupt being, motivated by selfishness, greed and lust. These evil impulses had to be restrained in order to prevent those of one social group from taking advantage of others who possess less power. So God provided the principle of government to keep men from destroying themselves in a "war of all against all."

What are the functions of the state? First, the state must provide and maintain law and order. It was ordained for man's good (Rom. 13:4), and ideally it allows believers to "lead a quiet and peaceable life, godly and respectful in every way" (1 Tim. 2:2). This implies freedom from strife, both internally (quiet) and externally (peaceable). The opposite of order is anarchy, an alternative which is totally unsatisfactory. It is more than coincidental that Paul referred to the Antichrist as "the man of lawlessness" (2 Thess. 2:3). When each man does what is right in his own eyes (Judg. 21:25) and has no consideration for his neighbors and their rights, chaos and confusion are bound to result. Anarchy is indeed a form of tyranny, and where an anarchic situation exists a tyrant will eventually exploit the opportunity to seize control and restore some form of law and order. Most theologians believe that government was instituted to enforce a certain minimum of public morality among individuals and groups so that order might prevail instead of confusion.

If the government refuses to fulfill its responsibility to uphold law and order, the Christian has the right to insist that it do its job properly. Paul and Silas, for example, were beaten and imprisoned by the authorities in Philippi for what allegedly was a breach of the peace. The next morning, when the magistrates ordered that they be quietly released, Paul demanded his rights as a Roman citizen. In what must be one of the earliest recorded instances of a sit-in, he declared: "They have beaten us publicly, uncondemned, men who are Roman citizens, and have thrown us into prison; and do they now cast us out secretly? No! let them come themselves and take us out" (Acts 16:37). In his last visit to Jerusalem Paul acted similarly when a Roman tribune was about to subject him to an illegal interrogation by scourging (Acts 22:24-29).

Another duty of the state is to provide justice, for without justice law and order are empty words. A major emphasis of the Old Testament is God's demand for justice. Establishing righteousness in society is associated with protecting and providing for the orphan, widow, stranger, poor and oppressed. This is the burden of Jeremiah's message to King Zedekiah in their confrontation over the issue of justice in the land (Jer. 22:3). In a similar manner Amos de-

nounced Kings Uzziah of Judah and Jeroboam II
of Israel:

> *Therefore because you trample upon the poor
> and take from him exactions of wheat, you
> have built houses of hewn stone but you shall
> not dwell in them; you have planted pleasant
> vineyards, but you shall not drink their wine.
> For I know how many are your transgres-
> sions, and how great are your sins—you who
> afflict the righteous, who take a bribe, and
> turn aside the needy in the gate. I hate, I
> despise your feasts, and I take no delight in
> your solemn assemblies. Even though you
> offer me your burnt offerings and cereal
> offerings, I will not accept them, and the
> peace offerings of your fatted beasts I will not
> look upon. Take away from me the noise of
> your songs; to the melody of your harps I will
> not listen. But let justice roll down like
> waters, and righteousness like an everflowing
> stream. (Amos 5:11-12, 21-24)*

A third responsibility of the political order is
to preserve liberty for its citizens. The Bible
makes plain that God intends for men to be free
(Jn. 8:32, 36) and that government is "God's
servant for your good" (Rom. 13:4). This means
that the state is obliged to keep men free from
oppression and provide the requisite measure of
peace and tranquility that will allow each person
to pursue his affairs unhampered. The late

Lutheran theologian Paul Elbrecht underscored the point that "government is to be good for people. It is not to be oppressive, mean, or vindictive. It is not to harass, frustrate, or pain" (Cf. Acts 4—5).[14]

What is the Christian's obligation to the state? The basic teaching of the New Testament is that the responsibilities of believers lie in two spheres—divine government and human government. Jesus' reply to the question "Is it lawful to pay taxes to Caesar, or not?" was, "Render to Caesar the things that are Caesar's, and to God the things that are God's" (Mk. 12:14-17). This was not a clever attempt to dodge the issue but an expression of the fundamental truth that Christians have obligations in both realms. Although their citizenship is in heaven (Phil. 3:20), they comprise that portion of the kingdom of God which is planted in the world. Even though Rome was a pagan, militaristic state, as long as it preserved justice and an orderly society it had a legitimate claim to the support of all its citizens, including the people of God.

In short, Christians are commanded to submit to the state because its authority is divinely sanctioned. In recognition of the divine source of the state, Christians are expected to give honor to its officials (Rom. 13:7; 1 Pet. 2:17) and pray for them since they are agents of God's purpose in the world (1 Tim. 2:1-2). Believers ordinarily should pay taxes for the support of the state and by implication should even render personal service if the opportunity presents itself (Rom. 13:6-7; Tit. 3:1). Finally, they are duty-bound to obey the regime—and not simply because the state has the power to enforce obedience. Christians comply with the law "for the sake of conscience" (Rom. 13:5) and "for the Lord's sake" (1 Pet. 2:13). For followers of Christ, almost all disobedience to the government, the structure of law and order, is disobedience to the will of God.

The realm of Caesar does not, however, have the ultimate claim on the allegiance of Christians. The power of the state must have a limit. A regime may become so corrupt as to forfeit its status as "the minister of God" and degenerate into a demonic beast that demands not only the obedience and submission of its citizens but also their worship. The biblical example of this is the totalitarian state of the Antichrist pictured symbolically in Revelation 13. Peter laid down the principle of resistance to such an order in his remarks to the Jewish Sanhedrin: "We must obey God rather than men" (Acts 5:29). Theologian George Ladd emphasizes forcefully that this means, "The state may never demand my total obedience. It may never infringe on my freedom to worship and serve God. Loyalty to the state is always conditioned by the higher loyalty to God."[15]

Thus, even though Christians have obligations in two realms, their final allegiance belongs to God. This extremely important point cuts the ground out from under the rationalization based on Romans 13 used by many German Christians to justify their participation in the Third Reich and its blatantly evil activities: "The government commanded me to do such-and-such, and I had to be subject to the powers that be since they are ordained of God" (or "orders are orders"). Such a statement is an unacceptable excuse for passivity in the face of monstrous political and social evils.[16]

Can a Christian be indifferent to political concerns? Those who downplay the necessity for Christian political involvement invariably mention the relative indifference of the New Testament to political matters. One may speculate, however, that God intended this silence in order to avoid incorporating into the Scriptures a first-century political legalism that in later times would have appeared to be rigid and irrelevant. One can observe that since the early believers expected the Lord to return momentarily, this effectively kept down much interest in current political, social and economic problems. Also, since the Roman system denied political power and responsibility to the great majority of its citizens, specific directions for political participation would have been meaningless in the context of the period. As a result, in Romans 13 Paul admonished Christians to follow no active political program but to remain passive to the demands of the Roman state.

In the twentieth century, however, the situation is far different. In the democratic and semi-democratic states that comprise much of the contemporary world the citizens themselves play a role in the selection of their rulers. All citizens share responsibility for the nature of the government and the laws which provide for justice. If the authority of the state is instituted by God and we are participants in determining its character, we are obligated to use our influence, voices and votes to promote principles of righteousness and justice in it.[17]

Should a Christian student get involved? This chapter has argued that in a democracy a Christian cannot afford to be indifferent to political concerns. Too much is at stake! In the following chapter the discussion will center on the need for Christian students to be involved personally in the major issues of the day.

chapter three

When Will Christians Stop Being Obscene?

One day several Kansas State University students lingered after class to discuss some of the issues raised by their professor's lecture on the history of Christianity. The animated discussion which followed over a cup of coffee in the Student Union centered on the ability of the Christian church in the past to reform itself in times of crisis and the desperate need for sweeping reform in the present day.

One of the students—a young man who had once held membership in a conservative church but had since dropped out—expressed his dissatisfaction with evangelical Christians for consistently supporting the status quo and resisting reform. What irritated him most, he said, was that so many believers were hung-up on what seemed to him to be minor taboos while they condoned the most outrageous sins in the political and social world around them. "Why is it," he asked the professor, "that Christians get up-tight about certain four-letter words and never open their mouths at all to protest the social evils of the world?" His teacher—who happened to be an evangelical—replied, "Well, I guess it's because they think those four-letter words are obscenities." "Obscenities," shouted the student, banging his hand on the table and attracting the attention of most of the other people in the room, "obscenities, the real obscenities are war, pollution, poverty, and racism! When will Christians stop being obscene?"[1]

The professor had no answer. The student was right! The question is valid: When will Christians stop being obscene and speak out against the great social and political sins of the day? Without condoning the use of four-letter words, cannot Christians recognize the infinitely more important task of addressing themselves to the issues of war and peace, pollution, poverty and racial justice?

Why Are Students Angry?/

There can be no mistake that we are living in a deeply troubled world. Christian students who are even half alive on the university campus are confronted at every turn with the issues of the hour. Many times these students are part of the problem when they should be part of the solution. Nearly every thinking person will admit the necessity of doing something to solve the problems—great and small—before it is too late.

Who can doubt that Western society is in trouble? Richard Nixon tells us so! Alvin Toffler tells us so! Martha Mitchell tells us so! Many of our most respected Christian leaders tell us so! In fact, today's world could be described by a line from Marc Connally's *Green Pastures*: "Everything nailed down is coming loose."[2]

The pressing need is for Christians to raise their voices and roll up their sleeves. Everybody seems to have legitimate questions—so few seem to have any valid answers. Christians do not have all the answers, but they certainly have some! As Senator Hatfield cogently pointed out in a commencement address at Fuller Theological Seminary in June, 1970: "I believe the evangelical community has as its most urgent task the developing of a responsible social and political ethic that takes with equal seriousness the truth of Christ's life and God's revelation of himself to man and the crisis confronting the social and political institutions of our age."[3] In other words, biblical perspectives need to be brought to bear on current social and political problems.

If Christians, especially the younger generation of evangelicals, do not speak up soon, they may lose both their right and their opportunity to do so. Followers of Christ on today's college campuses know that students are angry, and why. The tone and tenor of this anger is expressed clearly in an excerpt from a speech by a student activist made at the height of the Vietnam War controversy. Listen to his moral outrage:

> *. . . to bomb more hell out of a tiny Asian country in one year than was bombed out of Europe in the whole second World War becomes "escalation." Threatening to burn and blast to death several million civilians in an enemy country is called "deterrence." Turning a city into radioactive rubble is called "taking out" a city. A concentration camp (already a euphemism for a political prison) becomes a "strategic hamlet." A comparison of the slaughter on both sides in a war is called "kill ratio." Totaling up the corpses is called "body count." Running the blacks out of town is called "urban renewal." Discovering ingenious new ways to bilk the public is called "market research." Outflanking the discontented employees is called "personnel management." Wherever possible, hideous realities are referred to by cryptic initials and formula-like phrases: ICBM, CBR, mega-*

deaths, or "operation" this, "operation" that.[4]

Unfortunately, these bitter words contain too much truth for thinking Christians to gainsay them.

Students have come to see that many of those who constantly warn Americans against the threat of "godless, materialistic communism" are themselves just as godless and materialistic as the communists. Many young people are repelled by a society which deliberately manipulates human behavior for profit, even to the point of purposely making people feel uneasy about how they smell. Is not this economic determinism of the worst sort? Young men and women in increasing numbers are speaking against crass businessmen who use sex to sell merchandise, many times by attempting to create anxieties about sex and then playing on these anxieties to sell their products. Many Christian students were shocked and angered when they heard the President of the United States describe Neil Armstrong's 1969 moon-landing as a feat exceeded only by God at creation.

This is not to say that the average college student is some kind of left-wing radical bent on the destruction of the country's current political system. Recent studies show that this is not true, concluding that the large majority of students are not sympathetic with radical doctrines and tactics. But these same surveys and polls reveal that increasing numbers of college young people are discontented with the way the country is run, disillusioned by the values of the ruling authorities and deeply disturbed by the contradictions they see between an affluent society and the evils of war, pollution, racism and poverty.[5]

Today's youth are coming to reject materialism and commercialism as the chief ends of society. In ever growing numbers, the young in Western countries feel there must be other motivations than profit. Along with this change in perception of values is an increasing understanding that today's problems demand involvement and concern. As one bumper sticker puts it: "Support Your Local Planet." Surely Christians can understand this renewed interest among young people for answers to questions involving the worth and purpose of human life. These are spiritual concerns, and the ultimate answers to them are spiritual—in the fullest Christian sense of the word.

Christians and the Great Issues/
The most revealing fact about today's political and social problems is that they nearly all contain moral and spiritual dimensions. No evangelical Christian of any age group can ignore this.

Christianity is not something which can be compartmentalized and sealed off from the rest of life. It never has been and never can be "purely personal" because it has to do with mankind. Thus, a myriad of political and social questions —large and small—are of legitimate concern for Christians. Looming large among these are what might be called the great cosmic issues of our time, our modern-day "Four Horsemen of the Apocalypse," namely, poverty, racism, war and pollution.[6]

What have Christians done about these great overriding issues? Have they ignored these momentous moral questions? The answer is that many Christian leaders in public life have tried to do something about them. Although a number of statesmen could be mentioned, four impress the authors as outstanding examples of men moved by religious convictions to act in these areas of concern with considerable effectiveness.

The first of these is a former lieutenant governor of Illinois, Paul Simon. An active member of both the Lutheran Church—Missouri Synod and the Democratic Party, Simon has long been involved with the problem of poverty in the United States and elsewhere. He has expressed his concern that the United States has the ability to feed the world and yet apparently lacks the will to stop squandering its abundance and make its affluence available to more of its own population. By focusing attention on full Christian stomachs, he has sought to make many complacent evangelicals of "Middle America" more aware of their social responsibilities, both in Illinois and throughout the world.

Writing on this subject for his denomination in a study book entitled *The Christian Encounters a Hungry World,* Simon asserts:

> *God has provided adequately for the human beings on earth, but we fail to distribute and use what He has given us. It is just that simple. And no group on earth has a greater imperative to do something about it than people who call themselves Christians.*[7]

During his years as a state legislator and as lieutenant governor, Simon consistently supported programs aimed at alleviating the plight of the poor in Illinois. On the national level he has endorsed most of the current attempts to break the poverty cycle in America, including intelligent proposals made by both major parties.

A statesman of a different political persuasion from Simon with an equally deep concern for the poor is Republican congressman from Minnesota, Albert H. Quie. A committed Christian lawmaker, Quie belongs to the American Lutheran Church and is considered a practicing evangelical politician. In a succinct statement of his philosophy on Christian involvement he pointed out that "everybody must share his faith. We do whether we realize it or not. People expect good things from you as a Christian, and if they don't see good things, then your witness is negative."[8] As a high-ranking member of the House Education and Labor Committee, he has played a major role in shaping educational legislation during the last decade. Quie also co-authored the Republican alternative to the War on Poverty program, known as the Opportunity Crusade.

In his poverty proposals, as well as in his speeches and voting on welfare legislation, he has stressed that the poor themselves must have a real voice in planning, policy formation and program implementation. He believes strongly in community involvement and has sought to convince his colleagues that mere paternalistic government action on behalf of the poor is grossly inadequate to reverse the widening gulf between the poor and affluent in America. This is exemplified by the Quie Amendment to the poverty legislation of 1966, which earmarked at least one-third of the seats on local community action boards for representatives of the poor, chosen by residents of impoverished areas.[9] Like Paul Simon, Albert Quie has allowed his Christian faith to sensitize his conscience on moral issues and has acted on this basis.

A third illustration of how Christian convictions have served as a motivation for action, this time in the area of race relations, is Congressman John B. Anderson of Illinois. He was elected to the House of Representatives in 1960 and is now the third-ranking Republican member of that body. He is also an active layman in the Evangelical Free Church.

In April, 1968, Anderson was faced with what he later called "the single most dramatic incident of my years in Congress, and a crisis of Christian conscience."[10] Earlier, the House of Representatives had passed a mild civil rights bill, which the Senate then amended to include an open housing clause. This clause provided for federal penalties against anyone who refused to rent or sell property to another person because of his race, color or creed. When the Senate and House pass different versions of a bill, the customary procedure is to send it to a House-Senate conference, where the legislation is modified and made acceptable to both bodies.

However, on April 4, Dr. Martin Luther King, Jr. was assassinated, and a wave of racial violence swept across the United States. This lent urgency to the passage of a civil rights bill, and several House members wished to bypass the conference committee and accept the strong Senate version of the legislation. The House Rules Committee, to which Anderson belonged, was faced with the decision of whether to recommend passage of the Senate bill or to remand it to conference where the open housing provisions almost certainly would be watered down or even eliminated. Two years earlier Anderson had voted against a similar bill and many of his constituents were urging him to reject the new one. This time, however, he decided to support open housing legislation.

Anderson gives four reasons for his change of attitude. First, several witnesses at the Rules Committee hearing on the bill argued convincingly that the bill would serve as an important symbol to the black community of America's intent to go forward in the endeavor to create a free and open society where no man would be treated differently because of his skin color, religious beliefs or national origin. Moreover, the Report of the National Advisory Commission on Civil Disorders, which had been issued the month before, had shown that in every instance of racial violence in the previous two years, poor housing had been a significant factor in the total discontent of the black community. A third consideration was that some of his black constituents had informed him of their extreme difficulties in finding adequate places to live.

But the following reason, which he relates in his book *Between Two Worlds,* was more compelling than any other:

> *There came to bear in my thinking the realization that as a Christian—as one who believes*

that God created all men in His own Image, and of one blood; and as one who believes that the Son of God brought His message of salvation without regard to race, color, or ethnic background—I had to be willing to give up age-old prejudices, even to the point of subordinating something as fundamental as the right of contract to the even more fundamental principle of human rights. After many moments of prayer, meditation, and careful consideration of my responsibility as a Christian, I concluded that I could do nothing less than cast my vote in support of legislation which was admittedly sweeping in its ramifications, but which seemed justified not only by the urgency of the hour, but by even more basic considerations of human rights and human dignity.[11]

At the crucial Rules Committee meeting, Anderson joined seven Democrats in an eight-to-seven vote against sending the bill to conference. The bill then went to the House floor where the Illinois congressman gave an impassioned speech in favor of its passage. It passed— and was forwarded immediately to President Lyndon B. Johnson for signature as the Civil Rights Act of 1968. His one vote—dictated in the last analysis by the demands of his evangelical conscience—had made the difference in the Rules Committee and saved the bill from almost certain oblivion.

The fourth example of a Christian leader whose religious beliefs have directly influenced his actions on a major moral issue is Senator Mark O. Hatfield. A well-known Baptist lay leader, he was one of the first prominent political figures to speak out against American involvement in the tragic Vietnam conflict.

While he was governor of Oregon, he delivered the keynote address at the Republican National Convention at San Francisco in July, 1964, and spoke critically of the "war without a name." In 1965 and 1966, Hatfield was able to express even more forcefully his disapproval of the bloodletting in Southeast Asia. At the national governor's conferences in both those years, the states' chief executives were asked to endorse President Johnson's policies. Each time Hatfield cast the only vote against the administration.

Because of his Vietnam stance he faced a difficult campaign for election to the Senate in 1966. He was successful, however, and he used his position in Washington to push all the harder for ending the war. Perhaps his most noteworthy action was sponsoring a resolution with Senator George McGovern calling for an immediate end to American involvement.[12]

In an interview in *HIS* magazine published in 1967, Senator Hatfield was asked, "Does your peace emphasis on Vietnam stem from Christian convictions?'' His reply was candid and revealing:

My views are naturally influenced by my beliefs, by my faith, because no man can isolate or divide himself into tight little compartments that do not relate to one another. . . .

I have a feeling clearly that God created every human being on this earth in His own image and I hate to see the cheapness of life, the awesome loss of life through starvation or through war. I just cannot accept the idea that ultimate victory will be achieved by killing more people, killing more people, and killing more people.

I think we should take peace, prosperity, and food and love to these people. Paul teaches us that love is the most powerful instrument in the world. I think it is far more powerful than the atomic bomb, and we ought to use our genius and our ingenuity to find an honorable way to solve this problem. . . .

We have a responsibility to share the blessings that God has given us. Our material possessions, our wisdom, our education, are all things that we must share with other people because we are all our brother's keeper. I would much rather be a keeper than a destroyer, and that to me is what America is doing today, destroying people.[13]

One of Hatfield's most powerful speeches was the address which he gave at Fuller Seminary in 1970. In ringing tones the Oregon lawmaker declared concerning war and peace:

It is morally indefensible that our involvement in Southeast Asia should be justified on the basis of national pride or to avoid national humiliation. The more we do so, the less we have to be proud about. A nation that can turn from its past ways, admit its error and truly seek a new path—that nation can discover a true greatness of spirit. . . .

I cannot understand how a Christian community can abide these evils without at least asking the questions which need to be asked and without coming to at least some rudimentary and tentative responses to these questions. Let us each discover how we must obey the command of Christ when he instructs us to be his peacemakers.[14]

A fourth issue of the greatest magnitude now facing mankind is pollution. Francis Schaeffer and a number of other evangelical spokesmen have recently addressed themselves to the ecological crisis and pointed out biblical guidelines which, if followed, would bring "substantial healing" and restoration. In *Pollution and the Death of Man*, Schaeffer stresses the Christian doctrine of creation and the restorative power of the gospel as the basis for Christian action in this realm.[15]

Several evangelical legislators have joined with a host of other concerned lawmakers in a concerted effort to correct ecological abuses. Among these is Congressman Quie, who bases his support for environmental protection on the doctrines of creation and Christian stewardship. Quie believes that the pollution problem must be solved by a balanced and cooperative approach, one which involves the individual, his community and government. He feels that Christians cannot simply be *against* pollution—which is akin to being against sin—but that they must implement their concern with careful, positive action at all levels. When government is used, Christians should look closely at the "delivery method" of the solution and become involved in the mundane aspects of pollution control as well as in the more glamorous crusade against this evil. Too many Christians, he observes, simply do not want to participate in the hard work and sustained effort necessary to solve this staggering problem.[16]

Both Quie and Congressman John Anderson supported the Clean Water Act of 1972, which included funds for local sewage treatment plants to return nearly pure water to the nation's streams and lakes. When the President vetoed this bill—for his own good reasons—both congressmen felt strongly enough about this piece of environmental legislation to vote to override the presidental veto. Considering the nature of national politics and their party affiliation, this was an act of considerable Christian courage.

The deeds of these four leaders testify that some Christians have not ignored the great cosmic issues of our day and serve as a challenge to Christian young people to take a stand as well. If their elders continue to remain silent on these obscenities, then evangelical Christian students have a special obligation to sensitize them to these pressing problems and to prod them into action.

The Need for Practical Reform/
Equally important and often overlooked by Christians and non-Christians alike are the less grandiose issues which touch all citizens at the level of day-to-day political activity. Christian students need to be aware of these areas of political and social concern and to take positive action to bring about practical reforms at every level of government—local, state and national. The need for practical reform is overwhelming and not all areas needing attention can be discussed. Hopefully, a few examples will help Christian students see some of the bread-and-butter issues of today's democratic politics more clearly.

One major reform with which Christian students need to lend a hand is helping to curb the excessive influence of the rich in politics—both within and without the formal political process. This is not to say that rich people in general or rich Christians in particular should be excluded from public life. They certainly should not. The point is that in a democracy talented people from every sector of society should be able to participate in politics and hold public office. This is not the case in America, Great Britain and most of the Western democracies today.

It seems to be more difficult nowadays for moderate income people to run for public office and next to impossible for a poor person to do so. Some time ago Will Rogers wryly observed, "Politics has got so expensive that it takes lots of money to even get beat with."[17] This is even more true today at every level of government. The 1972 presidential campaign is a good example of the enormous amount of money now needed to elect someone to the highest office in the land. Present-day Abraham Lincolns have little likelihood of ever seeing the political light of day. Many people feel that there are only two ways for candidates to achieve high elective office in America: (1) be rich or (2) "sell" themselves to some well-heeled interest group or rich individual.

At the state and local levels the situation is

equally critical. Most small towns are run by a so-called power elite, usually consisting of ten or twelve of its most wealthy businessmen. The majority of American cities are controlled by big business or, in some instances, by some other powerful interest, like a political machine or a syndicate of gangsters. The majority of governors and many of those who sit in the state legislatures are themselves men of wealth or are closely controlled by men of wealth.[18]

Ordinary people are fed up with this situation, and perhaps have been for some time. They are weary of being pushed around at the local level by a small, privileged elite. They are tired of paying taxes to subsidize those rich, who elude their fair share of the burden of government through tax loopholes and other means. They are losing patience with a system which allows banks and loan companies to charge exorbitant interest rates in order to make money they do little to earn, thus keeping the average American in continuous debt most of his adult life. They are increasingly irked at having to supply the muscle and guts for an economy in which they feel they have a diminishing stake because of inconclusive wars they cannot understand and an inflation which daily robs them of their buying power.

The voice of the little people of America was expressed in a 1972 cartoon in which a

housewife is talking to someone on the telephone. She sits in a chair with arm in sling and
head bandaged, and her husband stands beside
her reading the help-wanted ads in the local
paper. She says to her friend on the phone:
"Everything's fine. Last week my boy was
wounded in the Vietnam Peace; yesterday I was
mugged on the streets that are Free of Fear; and
today my husband was laid off in the New
Prosperity."[19]

Who better than Christians can understand
and respond to the need to curb the inordinate
influence of the wealthy in government since
they know that God's Word abounds with concern for all people and not just the economically
powerful? Who better than evangelicals can
understand and respond to the plight of ordinary people in the world today since they themselves historically have smarted under the scorn
of the establishment and its abuse of power?
Who better than Christians in college can understand and respond to the need for all people to
be more fully and sympathetically represented
in the halls of government since they are close to
the issues of representation and involvement on
campus? Christians can do a great deal to curb
the influence of the wealthy if they simply will
apply biblical principles to the problem. When
they do, they will find that Moses and the
Prophets and Jesus and Paul were all on the side

of the poor, the down-trodden and the unheard. What could be more natural than for Christian students to make such causes their own?

A second pressing need in the political and social world is for judicial and legal reform. Courts need to be upgraded and enlarged, and the flow of cases expedited. Likewise, laws need to be updated and recast in terms understandable both to citizens at large and to public officials. Laws need to be written which carry out the intent of the legislators who passed them rather then become the object of legal games by expert lawyers skilled at freeing obvious lawbreakers on technicalities.

Most of all, the legal systems in many Western nations need to be revised so that the concept of "equality before the law" becomes more of a reality. Once again, the influence of the rich needs to be diluted and the interests of low and moderate income people protected. And just laws need to be enacted which safeguard the basic human rights of all men to "life, liberty, and the pursuit of happiness." As black evangelist Tom Skinner has pointed out so well:

Laws must be passed to create a climate for justice. Laws do not create a climate for love. But, then, laws are not intended to do that. From a scriptural point of view it is love which transcends law and not law which transcends love. The truly Bible-oriented man seeks always to balance love and justice, there being no contradiction between the two concepts.[20]

Creating a climate of justice in the land is a worthy goal for Christian students who claim to be followers of the Just God.

A last example of an area which needs practical reform is restoring confidence in government at all levels—a very real need yet perhaps the most difficult of all reforms to implement. In the last decade, trust in government leaders has eroded seriously in most Western nations for a variety of reasons. In the United States, it has been largely the Vietnam War with all of its attendant official lying which has made more and more young Americans skeptical about the trustworthiness of government pronouncements. From the hacks in many state and local governments to the outmoded seniority system in Congress, a great leadership crisis has descended upon the land. In Britain and America, in Canada and France, in most countries of the West, really outstanding leaders seem difficult to find in places of power in the decision-making process. Where are the Jeffersons, the Lincolns and the Churchills the democracies now so desperately need?

Christian students can help provide some of the new leadership which will be required if democracy is to survive the present crisis. They can support the first-rate leaders who presently are grappling with the difficult problems of the hour, and they can help identify and elect other high-caliber men of integrity to serve with them. They can commit themselves to work to defeat public officials who lie to the people and who cannot be trusted to place the welfare of all Americans above their own or those of some vested interest. Who is better suited to implement this kind of needed reform than those individuals whose Master exalted truth and was the Truth (Jn. 8:32; 14:1-6)?

Perhaps the real tragedy which a discussion of this kind reveals is not so much that evangelicals of the present generation have done little about social and political problems but that so many believers do not even know they exist! Is this true of Christian students as well? Can it be true that the current upsurge of interest in Christianity on the college campuses has overlooked the social dimension of the gospel? Are Christians at the universities neglecting to apply the whole gospel—one which includes love of neighbor as well as love for God? Do campus believers spend too much time majoring on minors while great problems slowly but surely devour the civilized world? Are evangelicals in their concern for decent language guilty of neglecting the supreme obscenities of war, poverty, pollution and racism, as well as the multitude of lesser social and political problems which so desperately need their attention?

Most concerned students respond to the sentiments of the great seventeenth-century poet and preacher John Donne. Do you as a Christian?

> *No man is an* Iland, *intire of it selfe; every man is a peece of the* Continent, *a part of the* maine; *if a* Clod *bee washed away by the* Sea, Europe *is the lesse, as well as if a* Promontorie *were, as well as if a* Mannor *of thy* friends *or of* thine owne *were; any mans* death *diminishes* me, *because I am involved in* Mankinde; *And therefore never send to know for whom the* bell *tolls; It tolls for* thee.[21]

Are you involved in mankind? Can any Christian escape the bell's toll? When *will* Christians stop being obscene?

chapter four

Why Do Jerry Rubin and Richard Nixon Think Today's Campus Is Important?

Part of John Donne's "maine" is today's university campus. This is one of the few points upon which Jerry Rubin and Richard Nixon agree.

Rubin and Nixon View the Campus/

Jerry Baby digs the campus but not the university. He spends a major share of his now almost forgotten book *Do It!* (published by the bourgeois firm of Simon and Schuster) exalting the freedom and reality of nonstudent life on and near campus while berating those stupid enough to remain in school. At the same time he calls upon the unliberated student to turn the university into a guerrilla stronghold which will eventually bring the establishment to its knees:

The class struggle begins in class. . . . We are going to invade the schools and free our brothers who are prisoners. We will burn the buildings and the books. We will throw pies in the faces of our professors. We will give brooms and pails to the administrators so they can be useful and sweep the place up.

The war on the campuses is similar to the war in Vietnam: a guerrilla people's war. By closing down 100 universities in one day, we, the peasants, can level the most powerful blow possible against the pigs who run American society. We'll force the President of the United States to come on his hands and knees to the conference table. We're using the campus as a launching pad to foment revolution everywhere.[1]

Rubin feels the campus is important not only because he so passionately hates it and all it stands for but also because he sees it as the springboard to a Yippie-style anarchist revolution.

Richard Nixon thinks the campus is important, too. And he agrees that it should be a source of change in society, but change of a far different sort than that envisioned by Rubin. Mr. Nixon paid visits to a number of college campuses during his first years in the White

House, mostly to schools where his aides felt he would encounter a minimum of student hostility. Even granting that the President made these trips to the nation's campuses partly for purposes of political gain, this in itself reveals that he believes the good will of college students is important to his own continuance in power. Also, he genuinely seems to think that the future of America depends upon the political bent of today's students.

In a controversial speech Mr. Nixon gave at Kansas State University on September 16, 1970, as part of the Landon Lectures, he addressed himself to the political importance of youth in the continuing quest of the so-called American dream:

The great strength of this nation is that our young people, the young people like those in this room, in generation after generation, give the nation new ideas, new directions, new energy. . . . As I speak in the heart of America, I can truly say to you here today you are the heart of America—and the heart of America is strong. The heart of America is good. The heart of America is sound. It will give us—you will give us—the sound and responsible leadership that the great promise of America calls for—and in doing so, you will give my generation what it most fervently hopes for: the knowledge that your generation will see

*that promise of the American dream ful-
filled.*[2]

From the foregoing it is obvious that both Mr.
Rubin and Mr. Nixon are intensely interested in
today's college campus, and for basically the
same reasons. Rubin sees revolutionary cadres
coming from this source, marching forth to
change society for the good. Nixon sees sturdy
soldiers of the establishment coming from this
source, marching forth to change society for the
good. But what lies beyond and beneath the
concern for the campus which these two politically perceptive men and others like them dis-
play? Why have college students within the last
decade become so important to the politicians?
This question deserves further examination.

The Universities As Political Focal Points/

It has long been common knowledge that the
university constitutes a unique subculture in any
society in which it exists. Always a place of
learning and sometimes even of bizarre new
ideas and avant-garde behavior, the university of
the past fulfilled an important political role as
the main critic of its society. However, this critical function was deemphasized in the twentieth
century, especially in the years following World
War II in the United States and elsewhere. More
and more the major function of the university
became that of providing a place to train for a

job, secure the necessary credentials for a professional career or earn a degree in order to grease
the skids of upward social mobility. Although
none of these goals is in itself undesirable or
bad, these goals historically were not the main
reasons for the existence of the university.

The reaction to a variety of factors both internal and external to the college campus came in
the 1960s. Many of the external factors have
been discussed already: the Vietnam War, the
civil rights movement, dissatisfaction with the
post-World War II drive for affluence, the redis-
covery of the poor and increasing signs of serious ecological problems.

The dam broke when students began to in-
quire into the role of the university as a recruit-
ing base for the much discussed military-indus-
trial complex. They started raising fundamental
questions about the real purpose of the university as an institution of higher learning and critic
of society at large. What happened to its alleged
objectives of asking the liberating questions
of life and promoting learning for learning's
sake?[3]

This internal unrest, coupled with the growing
external political and social pressures of the decade, led an increasing number of college students
in the 1960s to embrace fervently the ideals of
both a liberal education and liberal democracy,
and to become politically involved. As graduate

speaker Weldon Levine noted at the June, 1969, Harvard Law School commencement, "You have convinced us that equality and justice were inviolable concepts, and we have taken you seriously."[4]

In specific terms, there are a number of reasons why today's universities are the focal point of so much political action and attention. Some of these are more true of the average state school than of private institutions, but most apply to both. The Christian student should be aware of these reasons and take them into consideration as he seeks to determine in what way and to what extent God would have him get involved. They will help him see that, as far as politics is concerned, he is where the action is!

First, there is the obvious fact that public universities are sponsored, financed and controlled to some degree by the state. Continuing public support means continuing—in some places revived—public interest and accountability. Even private schools experience this political phenomenon to a certain extent in their relationships with donors and denominational contributions. It is not altogether unheard of in Christian circles for church-connected colleges to feel political pressure and ire from the money-paying constituency. In other words, part of the political flap on campuses today can be traced back to that age-old principle of "he who pays the piper calls the tune."

Second, universities are deeply involved in current politics because students, faculty and politicians seem to have rediscovered Sir Francis Bacon's famous seventeenth-century dictum that "knowledge is power." As a number of modern-day political scientists have observed, knowledge is the capital required by the post-modern industrial society. Universities are knowledge factories and as such have come to play as major a role in contemporary life as banks did at an earlier stage in American history. Given the nature of American life today, universities could hardly expect to be crucial to the nation's economic system without also being central to its politics.[5]

Third, since their founding in the Middle Ages, universities have served as critics of society. In twentieth-century America, this critical function was subverted by more utilitarian concerns. In recent years, however, it has been revived with renewed vigor and sometimes reckless abandon. Today's typical college is a little enclave of outsiders living as a separate and usually transient society in the midst of another America. It was really only a matter of time before the members of the supportive society on the outside realized that their children were being returned to them with an entirely different outlook on life than they had anticipated would be the case at the end of four years of traumatic experiences, high tuition and much book learning. This "Babylonian captivity of their children" by the professors has created widespread unrest among many working-class and middle-class parents who do not understand all this business about "doing your own thing," "finding yourself" and "being liberated from bourgeois provincialism." The only thing surprising about this reaction to the radical programming of students by the universities is that it was so long in coming. But when it came, it came with a vengeance and took many forms, including that of political reprisal.[6]

Fourth, the universities have become the principal problem-solving institutions in a problem-plagued society. Better bombs, a more rust-resistent wheat, a better grade of gasoline, a new strain of cattle which eats less but gains more, solutions to the mounting urban crime rate, streamlined business techniques—all of these have emanated in a large measure from our increasingly expert-laden universities for an expertise-demanding, technocratic state. The regime has called upon the universities and colleges to help and they have responded, but with deepening political involvement. And not the least important by-product of all this has been an increasing emphasis in the universities on research and a growing neglect of teaching students.

Fifth, the universities of America and Western

Europe have become increasingly unbalanced in their political composition. Today's American universities are not only politically involved; they are in many instances controlled, or at least heavily influenced, by the political left. Americans in the past have tolerated and even nurtured a university community slightly more liberal than the public at large. However, it seems that in recent years the college campus has veered more and more sharply to the left and become less and less tolerant of anything or anybody to the right of Fidel Castro. Increasing control by leftist elements has brought with it more political action and reaction on campus.[7]

Sixth, there are simply more students who desire to get a piece of the political action. This factor will become more evident and its implications as a focal point for campus political involvement more apparent now that eighteen-year-olds possess the right to vote.[8]

Finally, there is the growing feeling of estrangement between the university community and its constituency. This is in part because many professors and students would like to cease serving the technocratic state and return to the concept of a university as a place for "learning for learning's sake" and in part because of the growing public disillusionment with the previously accepted canon of liberal democracy that "education is the answer to all of our problems."

Taking all of the above factors into consideration, it is little wonder that those in the college community have been in the vanguard of the recent cutting issues. It was in a large measure professors and students who went to the American Southland to sit in at lunch counters, ride the buses and march to Selma with Dr. King. It was on the university campus where the first real brakes were applied to the Vietnam War. College students for the most part transformed Senator Eugene McCarthy from an enigmatic dreamer into a serious presidential candidate in 1968. And it is the university which is still the single most important force in the present drive for significant reform in Western democratic politics.

Why Are College Students Politically Important?/

Christian students may not be fully aware of or completely comprehend all of these reasons why the university is now a major focal point of political involvement, but in a general way they sense that it is. If this political activism is to be turned into constructive and beneficial channels, and if the university is to be preserved as a place of truly independent thought and research, then evangelical Christian students had better get involved! For the same reasons that society at large needs their insights, concern and leadership, so does the college campus.

The involvement and concern of Christian students will be enhanced by a proper understanding of the important role that today's college generation can and does play in politics. In other words, Christian students in particular can better mobilize for action if they know why students in general are important.

There are a number of reasons for the growing political significance of today's college students. First and foremost is the sheer size of the student population, particularly because, as pointed out earlier in this chapter, students now have the franchise. Over nine million young people are now enrolled in America's institutions of higher learning, a greater number and a larger proportion than has been so engaged in any other nation at any time in the history of the world. This enrollment is expected to rise substantially higher by 1980 before it peaks.[9]

With the lowering of the voting age to eighteen in Great Britain in 1970 and the United States in 1971, young people can now have a decisive influence in the political affairs of those two nations. In America it is estimated that over twenty-five million new voters were old enough to cast ballots in 1972 who were not eligible to do so in 1968. Mr. Nixon's margin of victory over Hubert Humphrey in the 1968 presidential election was a mere 511,944 votes. A comparison of these two figures illustrates the kind of impact young voters could have on the choice of a President *if* they make the effort to go to the polls, *if* they really want to match their words with action and *if* they truly desire to change things for the better.[10] In any event, it seems clear that students can have a significant voice in future elections *if* they take the trouble to vote. Involved, articulate students can no longer be ignored by the nation's political leaders.

A second reason why college students are politically important is that they are the future leaders of society. This may sound trite to many young people, but nevertheless it is still true in most of the civilized countries of the world. This is not to say that college students are unimportant now or that they should forego political involvement until they are older. On the other hand, most people who are eighteen usually do grow older, and, as they grow older, they customarily move into places of greater and greater responsibility, commensurate with their talents and training. Eventually, most of today's student generation will move into key roles as "opinion-makers" and as such will become extremely important to the political future of their respective nations.

A third reason why politicians have discovered college students is that they recognize great potential in the energy and enthusiasm of

this age group. In current American politics the
accent has been on youth since 1960 when John
F. Kennedy demonstrated how this vitality
could be channeled into a political campaign.
The real strength of any political party or movement is at the grassroots level where shirtsleeve
precinct work makes the difference between victory and defeat. Every candidate needs dedicated workers who are willing to do the hard
and unglamorous labor in the wards and pre-
cincts. Behind every state-wide elected candidate
there are thousands of dedicated workers. These
helpers at the local level are especially important
to candidates with limited financial resources
who may challenge the powerful, well-heeled
representatives of the power structure.[11]

The idealism of the average college student is
another reason why the politicians stalk the college campuses looking for support. Both Jerry
Rubin and Richard Nixon express this motivation for their attraction to the universities. Most
collegians are not yet committed to the status
quo and have not been bought out by the establishment. Most young people are idealistic and
have not been morally blunted or given themselves over to a cynical outlook on life. They can
bring to politics and politicians the freshness
that comes with this kind of outlook. Both conservative and liberal politicians are touched by
youthful idealism and often welcome it. This

makes an impact upon the leaders of any government and at least challenges them to rethink positions on issues which they may have too long taken for granted.

Finally, college students of today are important for the political future of the world because so many of them are at a crucial age for the formulation of political awareness and ideals, party loyalties and a general overall philosophy of life. In fact, most of the momentous decisions of an individual's life are made or intensified during the college experience: marriage, vocation, religion and basic political outlook.

The Christian Student's View of the Campus/
Political awareness comes almost automatically to anyone who is half alive on today's campus. It is difficult to avoid the great issues of the day because they stare students in the face in class, at the Union, in the dorm and even at the local tavern. Speakers challenge, posters announce, student leaders harangue, and the rank and file listen. Although most students do not identify with either of the two major parties, the vast majority of those who do make some sort of political commitment during student days stick with it for the remainder of their lives.[12]

Most important of all for Christian students is the fact that their classmates during college days are making important decisions about their basic philosophy of life—searching for a satisfying world view which will give meaning and purpose to their existence. They are looking for a professor or a fellow student they can respect and trust, a human being who is as concerned as they are about life and its problems. Many of them, in the full flush of youthful idealism, arc tired of sham and hypocrisy and are looking for reality in both the political and the social realm. Among other things, large numbers are looking for somebody who both preaches and practices his ideals.

Perhaps an excerpt from some free verse written by a co-ed at Arizona State University best conveys this feeling of search and expectation. In an item submitted to the ASU student newspaper she wrote:

I'm tired, tired of puppets instead of people,
Of persons who drop soliloquies carefully
      labeled intelligence.
I'm tired of cynics who call themselves
      realists,
Tired of minds rotting in indifference,
Of people bored because they're afraid to care;
I'm tired of people who have to be entertained,
Of girls proud of knowing the score and
      snickering about it;
I'm tired of sophisticated slobs,
Tired of people with nothing better to do
      than glue their days together with alcohol.

I'm tired of people embarrassed at honesty,
   at love, at knowledge.
Tired, yes . . . very tired.[13]

It seems apparent that on a university campus teeming with thousands of serious, questing students, genuine followers of Jesus Christ who also happen to be college students cannot avoid being involved politically in one way or another. The opportunities are virtually unlimited. Rank-and-file collegians are looking for something that will satisfy the whole man. Why not give them Jesus *and* a personal example of somebody of contemporary flesh and blood who like Christ cares for other people and their needs? Christian students should join Jerry Rubin and Richard Nixon in their concern for the college campus. The campus is important!

The next chapter will discuss ways of putting this great political potential on the campus to work for the glory of God and the betterment of mankind.

chapter five

How Does Christian Concern Translate into Political Clout?

Christian students are clearly in a favorable position to make their weight felt in the political process. The great influx of new voters into the electorate along with the growing emphasis upon youthful vigor in candidates for public office has vastly heightened the political importance of the younger generation. This is illustrated by the manner in which youthful figures, with their more flexible attitudes toward vexing political questions, are coming to play an increasingly significant role in public life, especially at the state and local levels.

Opportunities for Political Involvement/
Where should young persons begin? What oppor-

tunities are open to them? First of all, they must become informed about the vital issues of the day—both on the local and national levels. They should read newspapers, magazines and books, watch the many fine public affairs programs on television and take part in issue-oriented study groups. They ought also to scrutinize those who are running for public office in their area and find out what their stands are on major issues. In other words, they should try to determine which candidate would make the best public servant.

Second, they must vote on the basis of this carefully gathered information. The number of people who do not vote at all or who are ill-informed when they do cast their ballots is scandalous. Of all people, Christians should be the most diligent in carrying out this basic function of citizenship.

Third, the young person should plunge into the fray. He can become part of the regular party organization, a voluntary ad hoc campaign committee or the personal campaign staff of a candidate. He should not be deterred by the prospect of having to cooperate with people who may not be Christians and to identify with their concerns and purposes. After all, this does not necessarily mean that he must conform at all times to the spirit and practices of a political group and abandon his own principles. These three important instructions call for further explanation and amplification.

The student who wishes to approach political involvement intelligently must exercise care in choosing his sources of information. Since he cannot obtain firsthand knowledge about all the candidates and issues, he must rely upon others for data on which to make political judgments. Because all opinion-shaping agencies have their political biases, no single source of information is reliable by itself. The family, social club, gang at work, church, press, television, radio and motion pictures—all sift the political news and color it according to certain presuppositions. Thus a person must control the information he receives so that he will be exposed to several differing points of view. This problem is particularly acute for Christians since church leaders and religious journals have no special immunity from the diseases of unrecognized or deliberate biases in politics. The comments of Walfred Peterson, Professor of Political Science at Washington State University, regarding the bias of Christian spokesmen are particularly well taken:

> *Because they believe themselves to be striving disinterestedly for the common good and for God's will in the world, they run the special risk of the arrogance of assuming and implying that their opinion and their "facts" are preferred in the divine order of things.*[1]

For a democratic system to function properly, the voter must act on the basis of issues. Since voters determine the general policy of their state, what a candidate stands for and promises to do is far more important than the attractiveness of his personality. Peterson suggests that it is not easy to vote on the basis of judgments about political issues. For one thing, the nonpolitical affiliations of the candidate should not affect the voter's action. Simply because a particular contender for office professes to be a Christian is in itself not an adequate reason for other believers to vote for him. His stand on the issues should be the decisive consideration, not his religious connection.

Moreover, the candidate's party affiliation is not always an accurate guide to his political views. Each party has its "liberals" and "conservatives" while great variations exist in the political climate from one part of the country to another. Finally, a candidate should be judged primarily on public policy considerations, not on the quality of his private life. Christians especially must refrain from deciding for or against a candidate on the basis of some negative code of Christian ethics. Whether a man drinks or is divorced should be a secondary rather than a primary factor in evaluating his qualifications for public office.[2]

A common political misconception is that a single vote does not count for much. "What difference does it make if I don't get to the polls?" is a question heard over and over again by those active in politics. Yet history is replete with examples of where a few votes did, in fact, make a difference, and after a major election one frequently hears of a local contest that was decided by a single vote. Vance Hartke's narrow win in the 1970 Senate race in Indiana was by approximately one vote per precinct. College students engaged in getting voters out for Hartke that election day discovered firsthand how significant each vote can be. In 1960 President Kennedy's margin of victory over Richard Nixon in the popular vote was only 113,000 out of nearly sixty-nine million cast, less than one vote per precinct in the nation!

Interestingly enough, the classic story of the potential importance of one person's vote in a democratic society is that of an Indiana farmer named Henry Shoemaker. In 1842 he cast a vote breaking a tie for his state representative, who in the following year broke a tie in the voting for one of Indiana's United States senators. (At that time senators were chosen by state legislatures.) In 1845, the senator—Edward Hannegan—cast the deciding vote which brought Texas into the Union, and in 1846 broke the tie in the Senate on the issue of war with Mexico. Thus, farmer Shoemaker's one vote had a profound effect upon the shaping of American history.[3]

Unfortunately, the United States has had a particularly bad record in voter participation. In the presidential election of 1964, more than one-third of all Americans of voting age—about thirty-seven million—failed to exercise the franchise. President Dwight Eisenhower did not receive that many votes in 1952 or 1956. In the 1966 congressional elections, less than one-half of the eligible voters went to the polling places, while in primary elections the turnout was even lighter. This voter apathy means that a minority actually chooses the leaders who make the important decisions affecting every citizen in the society.

Worst of all is the abysmal voting record of American youth. In the 1964 election only fifty-two percent of those between the ages of twenty-one and twenty-five cast ballots, while fifty-seven percent of those over the age of seventy-five turned out to vote.[4] The failure of young people to exercise adequately the right of suffrage is a serious flaw in the American system and should be a matter of concern for every Christian. Whether this trend in the United States will be reversed, only time will tell.

Those young people who wish to extend their scope of involvement beyond that of being an informed voter have many opportunities open to them. They can volunteer at the local party headquarters to pass out literature, stuff envelopes, make neighborhood surveys, baby-sit for mothers on election day, transport voters to the polls and carry out many other tasks of a routine nature. They may join the campaign staff of a particular candidate and do the same kind of work for him. They may help out in voter registration drives—especially among those groups which hitherto have not been adequately represented in the councils of government. They can join the local Young Republican or Young Democrat club, or its campus counterpart, if such an organization exists. Further, they may be able to secure summer internships in the offices of legislators in the nation's capital or to find similar posts in government offices at the state or provincial level.

Some will even be tempted to run for office and this is especially praiseworthy. It is probably best for such people to start at the ground level and work up—to make a bid for election as a precinct committeeman, a delegate to a state party convention, or a member of a city or county council or school board. The experience they gain in these basic offices in the political system will assist them in sharpening their skills and perhaps enable them to aspire to higher posts. State and provincial governments offer some of the most challenging opportunities for Christians. The Christian officeholder at any level will be in a position to make unique contributions because of his faith.

Christian Contributions to Democratic Politics/

What do Christians have to offer the world of politics? What distinctive contributions can they make? First, biblically oriented Christians understand the need for *balance and moderation*. "Let all men know your forbearance" (Phil. 4:5) is the scriptural injunction. Both Peter and Paul stress self-control as a Christian virtue (Gal. 5:23; Tit. 1:8; 2 Pet. 1:6). Sir Frederick Catherwood, an evangelical who has had considerable experience in British politics, argues strongly that, to be effective, efforts to exert positive political influence must be aimed at the middle-of-the-road element which comprises the majority in most modern democracies.[5] Thus, genuine Christians are clearly in a better position to influence people than are extremists.

Believers can contribute a balanced perspective on both political and social action. They can show from the Scriptures that the humanistic, utopian dream of a better society constructed by the hand of man alone is a false hope. They know that sin and the potential for evil lurks in the breast of every man, and therefore politicians are imperfect beings, even when they may sincerely be acting on high ethical principles. Thus, Christians are protected from falling into either the left-wing trap of idealizing the dispossessed and downtrodden or the right-wing snare of confusing material benefits with spiritual well-being.

Further, believers possess a *social conscience* based upon the Word of God. They do not involve themselves in political and social life in order to save themselves or redeem the world, but rather they follow the divine commands to love their neighbor and seek his welfare. As Francis Schaeffer points out, love is "the mark of the Christian," and "we are to love our fellowmen, to love all men, in fact, as neighbors."[6] Hence, followers of Christ work in the world to make it a place where God's righteousness and love can be displayed and fundamental human justice maintained. They do this, not for hope of reward or the praise of men, but out of gratitude to the God who loves them and has provided for their salvation.

In addition, Christians bring to the political realm a *sense of integrity* that so often is lacking there. They recognize that certain absolutes underlie human society and that their lives must be brought into conformity with these absolutes. They have a firm commitment to truth and honesty in all aspects of interpersonal relationships. They will take stands on moral issues and affirm without hesitation that acts of the state which violate God's law are wrong. Although they are ready to negotiate and compromise on most political issues, they will not give in on the fundamental questions of right and wrong. They have the necessary spiritual tools to combat the tendency of politics to be "dirty."

Finally, Christians have the training and temperament to *look at issues and not men.* They realize from the Scriptures that God has made them stewards over the world which he created. God has provided political power as one implement for accomplishing this task, and Christians are expected to use this power to control governmental authorities and direct their efforts into proper channels. In short, they must exercise a *stewardship of influence.*[7] Christians are obligated to take the opportunity for political participation seriously. They should be sensitive to the working of the Holy Spirit in all aspects of their life, regarding no part of it lightly. This sense of responsibility, then, extends to the civic realm, and believers will seek divine direction with regard to voting and the possibility of even more active involvement in political affairs.

A Word of Caution/
Before they plunge unreservedly into the fray, however, Christians should be aware of the hard facts of democratic political life. It is not a bed of roses, and many a sensitive person has been crushed in the bitter clash of personalities and

rival power groups that characterize much of political life. A person who is forewarned about the pitfalls of civic involvement will be better prepared to cope with these difficulties as they arise and thereby be in a position to make a more meaningful contribution to the life of his nation.

The first problem is that of *compromise,* a thing that many Christians regard as evil and feel must be avoided at all costs. However, the principle of compromise is vital to the existence of human society. Social life is primarily the play and clash of interests, both of individuals and groups. If the persons and groups within society are unable to work out compromises with respect to their rights, the result will be unbridled individualism or anarchy. The alternative to negotiation and compromise is the coercion of the weaker by the stronger, in other words, tyranny. In order to have a functional democratic system, Christians in particular must recognize that no one can have his own way all the time.

A clear distinction must be made between the compromise of Christian convictions about fundamental moral issues that are based solidly upon biblical teaching and the compromise of personal opinions that are related to a person's interest groups. To illustrate, since the Bible teaches that human life is sacred, a believer serving on a city council would certainly support a measure designed to protect lives—for example, a strictly enforced fifteen-mile-per-hour speed limit in school zones when children are in the streets. On the other hand, he would not endorse on the basis of Christian convictions an action which reflected the desires of an interest group—for instance, rezoning a large tract of land set aside for residential purposes so that a group of developers can construct a shopping center. The former is clearly a moral question; if certain people oppose the speed limit because they have been caught in a radar trap, the Christian would have to resist them in order to protect the city's children from being killed or injured in accidents. The latter, however, is a matter of conflicting interests; the owners of an existing shopping center or a group of nearby homeowners may object to the rezoning measure. Before deciding upon a course of action, a Christian would have to weigh the various implications of the change and consider how it would affect the community he was elected to serve.

The operational idea of compromise is that in order to gain a majority of supporters for many measures, it is often necessary to make concessions. This is the way political life functions in a democracy. Legitimate forms of negotiation or conciliation and the sacrifice of a Christian principle are therefore two different matters.

Remember that godly men such as Joseph and Daniel served pagan rulers but stood by their convictions. The temptation to sin by compromise is no worse in politics than in any other walk of life, and, in this case as in all others, believers have been given the promise of spiritual help. The Word of God states clearly: "No temptation has overtaken you that is not common to man. God is faithful, and he will not let you be tempted beyond your strength, but with the temptation will also provide the way of escape, that you may be able to endure it" (1 Cor. 10:13).

The second difficulty is the *complexity of issues*. The politician is seldom able to provide answers that will satisfy everybody. Most political questions are characterized by large fuzzy, gray areas, and the politician frequently has to act on matters where he cannot determine whether a thing is absolutely right or absolutely wrong. As Baptist ethics professor William M. Pinson correctly observes, "Almost every vote, almost every action in the world of politics is an action that involves some wrong, a lesser of two evils." Fortunately, Christians who choose to participate in political life are not left to flounder helplessly. Pinson goes on to say:

> *The Christian, though he is concerned and tries the best he can, is set free, because he is not saved by doing the right. He is saved by*

living in faith. So if you are going to sin, sin for good. Throw yourself into an arena of life in which you are not going to know for sure that you are right. Prayerfully, thoughtfully, determinedly, honestly you throw yourself into it; and if you are wrong, there is confession and repentance and forgiveness and another try. The Christian is free to fail! That sets you free for politics.[8]

The third harsh reality is that politics is *slow, hard work*. Christians must recognize that far-reaching change seldom occurs overnight in a democracy. Political activity usually is tedious and seldom is rewarded with immediate results. Christians in politics will quickly learn that ideas do not sell themselves automatically and that they must toil to win others over to their position on an issue. Many times they will have to be satisfied with something less than they set out to do. The fact that Perry Mason and Matt Dillon can wrap it all up in an hour has little basis in the real world of politics. To imagine that simply getting involved will bring instant success and speedy solutions is not only a weak and egocentric approach to politics; it is also a dead end!

To use an illustration from the world of sports, it is easy to sit on the sidelines and criticize the quarterback and the offensive line. But it is quite another to take a place on the line and block that six-foot-four-inch, 250-pound hunk of pure beef on the hoof on the other side of the line—that veritable mountain of hostility, agility and mobility dedicated to tearing you into shreds of human confetti in order to get at the ball carrier and the ball. Applying this analogy to public affairs, it could be said that other forms of government are much easier than the democratic system, and require far less work and participation from the people. But if Christians feel that the democratic form of government is the best, especially since it allows greater expression of freedom than any other kind, hard work is the price all must pay for the maintenance of this system. If the people of God are not willing to shoulder the burdens of democracy, the hope for its survival is quite dim.

Finally, active political participation requires *intense personal self-sacrifice.* The work is often thankless and discouraging, and it sometimes means psychological strain and heartbreak for those involved in it. The problems are difficult, and, no matter what a politician does, invariably someone will be dissatisfied and complain about it. Every person in the community has the right to criticize the acts of any public official, and the critics have the advantage of hindsight, a privilege denied the decision-maker. The lament of most elected officials is, "When you are right nobody will ever tell you and when you are wrong everybody lets you know."[9]

From a personal standpoint, political endeavor places heavy demand upon one's time, family and financial resources. Many friends will automatically assume that an individual is in politics for some ulterior motive, and they will reveal this by the knowing look or sly remark. Others will look askance at the Christian in political life and accuse him of compromising and selling out the faith. At the same time, some of the established political hacks will anything but welcome the arrival of a neophyte who gives allegiance to higher principles than those of pure expediency or the path of least resistance.

The pitfalls of political participation are many, but then so are the rewards. In spite of the difficulties and hardships, Christians are able to bring about change and improvement in society through political action. There are numerous instances of statesmen and activists in both the past and present who, motivated and undergirded by a vital Christian faith, entered the political arena and achieved their goal of improving the quality of human existence. A look at some of these great leaders, their deeds and experiences, can serve as a powerful stimulus to today's Christian young people to get involved.

Christians Can Effect Change: The British Evangelicals/
An outstanding example of a Christian who did

not avoid political action to combat social evils is William Wilberforce. Elected to a seat in the British Parliament at the age of twenty-one, he was converted at twenty-six and devoted the rest of his life to combating the slave trade. From 1789 to 1791 Wilberforce and some associates worked on gathering data for a report on slavery and then introduced a bill for abolition of the trade. It lost decisively but he did not give up. He sponsored another abolition bill which passed, and the traffic in slaves by citizens of Great Britain was outlawed, beginning in 1808. Wilberforce and his allies then applied pressure both directly and through the British government to induce other European countries to join the ban on the trade in human beings and to permit the British navy to police the high seas in order to stop the traffic.

Since the colonial legislatures in the West Indies refused to do anything to improve the lot of blacks there, the abolitionist forces directed their focus on the institution of slavery itself. Because Wilberforce was aging, the mantle of parliamentary leadership fell upon a young businessman who had turned to Christ, T. Fowell Buxton. Although originally a crusader for prison reform, Buxton in 1822 decided to make abolition his main interest. In 1823 he joined Wilberforce and gradually assumed the place of primary leadership in the movement to end slavery. More than ten years later, after a long period of public agitation and legislative initiative, Buxton was successful. Thanks largely to the dogged determination and incessant pressure brought to bear by Buxton and Wilberforce, Parliament finally yielded. In one stroke in 1833 it passed a bill liberating over 700,000 slaves in the British Empire, thus capping the generation-long efforts of two outstanding Christian laymen who were driven by an evangelical conscience to seek an end to the degrading institution of human slavery.

Another English evangelical who was impelled by his faith to enter political life and work for the benefit of his fellow men was Anthony Ashley Cooper, the seventh Earl of Shaftesbury. A devout Christian, he entered the House of Commons in 1826 and made it his mission to advance both man's welfare and God's glory. In his sixty years in public life he operated on the principle that he would use the law to combat that which was morally wrong and to protect the oppressed and downtrodden in British society. His first legislative efforts were directed at improving the quality of the institutional care for the insane.

Much more significant, however, was his work on behalf of the industrial working class. Early in 1833 Shaftesbury assumed parliamentary leadership of the factory reform party and intro-

duced a bill to regulate child labor. Manufac-
turing interests succeeded in blocking it. But
immediately after this first failure, he was
named to head a royal commission of inquiry
into laboring conditions. This further sensitized
him to the desperate lot of the workers, and the
government was forced to move quickly to obtain a passage of a moderate factory reform bill
to avoid an even stricter one which Shaftesbury
was preparing. Even passage of this measure,
which banned children under ten from working
in textile mills, limited hours of work for those
under eighteen and provided for inspectors to
enforce the law, would possibly have failed if it
had not been for the energetic pressure tactics of
the evangelical bloc in Parliament. After this,
Shaftesbury became involved in the struggle to
obtain a ten-hour day for English workers and
was the moving spirit behind such a bill in 1847.

Perhaps his most famous endeavor had to do
with the British coal miners. This began when he
chaired a committee to look into the problem of
women and children working in the mines. The
committee report, officially presented in 1842,
revealed human misery so shocking in its nature
and extent that Shaftesbury easily convinced
Parliament to adopt a Mines Act that limited
child labor and banned women from the pits. He
also obtained legislation in 1851 to provide for
the inspection and registration of lodging houses

for workers and in 1864 to prevent children from becoming chimney sweeps. During the Crimean War he persuaded the British War Department to send out a commission to investigate conditions in the military hospitals and assisted in setting up that commission. A direct result of this activity was Florence Nightingale's famous reforms in the care of the sick and wounded on the battlefields which saved hundreds of lives.

Wilberforce, Buxton and Shaftesbury are three of the most notable examples of English evangelicals who became involved in politics. In spite of numerous setbacks and disappointments, through perseverance and hard work they obtained passage of legislation that improved the quality of life for people who were otherwise politically defenseless and at the mercy of a cruel and unjust social system. Historian Earle Cairns has correctly observed about these men: "The inspiration for their work was their faith, and apart from their personal faith in Christ as Saviour and a love for men as potential or actual sons of God one cannot explain their work."[10]

In an important study of social reform in nineteenth-century England, Kathleen Heasman shows that the great majority of the period's voluntary charitable organizations were evangelical in character and control.[11] These organizations set the pattern and suggested the lines of action that were later to be followed by the state social service in Britain. The evangelicals not only stressed individualistic social action by philanthropists and voluntary agencies but, led by Shaftesbury, they were active throughout the century on the legislative front as well. Recognizing that government action was necessary to eliminate the worst abuses in British society, they were not reticent about petitioning Parliament for laws to regulate factory conditions, prevent young girls from being sold into prostitution, provide better treatment for young criminals and protect seamen. They never felt that it was wrong for Christians to look to the state for assistance in implementing social reforms.

American Evangelicals and Political Action/
Numerous examples could be cited of American, as well as British, Christians who have spoken out against social evils and worked for change within the political system. A whole generation of abolitionists identified with churches in various denominations. Most of them were influenced by the hard-hitting antislavery and anti-racist preaching of Charles G. Finney, the major evangelist of the first half of the nineteenth century. Other Christian reformers, such as Frances Willard and D. L. Moody, worked in the temperance crusade and were successful in obtaining a legal ban against the manufacture and sale of

alcoholic beverages. Many of the early leaders in the social gospel movement were close to the orthodox tradition, especially Walter Rauschenbusch who believed in the need for personal regeneration as well as a program of social action. During the Progressive era of the early 1900s, their activities resulted in a significant amount of legislation which dealt with urban problems and political reform at state and local levels.

Goodwill Industries was founded in 1902 in the Methodist Church of Edgar J. Helms in Boston. Handicapped workers were employed in renovating old clothes, furniture and appliances for sale to poor people at low prices. The money raised was used to pay the handicapped. Today Goodwill Industries is one of the leading contributors to the rehabilitation and well-being of handicapped people in America.

William Jennings Bryan was the most distinguished Christian statesman of the early twentieth century. His forceful opposition to American overseas imperialism in 1900 and his commitment to the peace movement have been overlooked by most scholars, who only remember his pitiful showing at the infamous Scopes Trial in 1925. As Woodrow Wilson's secretary of state, Bryan was the prime mover behind some thirty conciliation treaties with other nations; these were designed to cool passions that normally would lead to international conflict. Further, he resisted pressures from those in high places who wanted the United States to intervene on the side of Britain and France in World War I and was forced to resign in 1915 because of his firm commitment to neutrality and peace. Bryan and others like him demonstrate that the evangelical social conscience was alive and well in early twentieth-century America.

How Can Christians Today Bring About Change?

Christians can bring about change today by various political tactics. The following cases illustrate what can be done at the level of the local church congregation, the community or town, the state or province, and finally the national government. First, what can a *local congregation* do? Foy Valentine, head of the Southern Baptist Convention's Christian Life Commission, relates how Leonard G. Broughton, pastor of a Baptist church in Atlanta, Georgia, applied pressure on city government to rectify a deplorable situation. A suburban area had been annexed to Atlanta, but nothing had been done to extend city services there. Typhoid fever germs got into the water supply of the new district, resulting in four deaths. The city authorities discussed the matter at length but did nothing about the emergency. At the same meeting the council voted $15,000 to pave the street in front of the home of one of Atlanta's most influential men.

Dr. Broughton was disgusted by the situation. On Saturday evening he called City Hall and said, "Tomorrow morning I want two of your men in my church." In the worship service next day he announced to his congregation: "I am asking you to let me keep until next Sunday morning the sermon topic which has previously been announced. Today I want to show you the Word of God regarding the emergency which troubles our city." Then he proceeded to show from the Bible how God created human bodies as well as human spirits, how he made all things for the benefit of man, how God's laws help mankind to live fully and completely, and how he is as eager for people to have good drinking water as he is for them to attend prayer meeting.

The minister noticed that even before he was half finished the message was hitting home. The two invited guests from the city administration were trying to hide behind the people in front of them. Before ten o'clock the next morning the necessary money had been voted to provide the water system and within thirty-six hours the typhoid epidemic had abated.[12]

The second example reveals what is possible at the *community* level. An energetic, young Christian educator, Dr. W. Richard Stephens, became involved in helping to organize a human relations commission in Terre Haute, Indiana, one of the state's largest university cities. He realized that the passage of the Civil Rights Act of 1964 would not in itself rid society of racism, especially at the local level. And so, motivated by a deep sense of Christian obligation to work for reconciliation and healing in a society torn by racial tensions, he and several colleagues pledged themselves to work within established governmental and religious agencies to implement the promises of the 1964 act. Their first step toward the elimination of racism was to secure the creation of an official human relations commission by the city.

Stephens' description and evaluation of the endeavor can best be presented in his own words:

Following several sessions in which we developed our strategy to get a human relations commission plan before the city council, our small integrated group of social reformers held a number of meetings with various people in the city. . . . When our activities were eventually reported in the news media, opposition began to mount from all quarters. Some successful efforts were made to fragment our forces, but after many hours of time spent in meetings and panel discussions and after scores of telephone calls, the city council finally voted to establish a human relations commission. Though it was far from a model ordinance—the commission lacked an adequate budget and had only minimal enforcement powers—the new body began its work with diligence.

What did the Terre Haute Human Relations Commission accomplish? During the first three years of its existence I had opportunity as one of its members to observe its workings from the inside. The commission brought together those black citizens caught in the ghetto with their white neighbors in middle class suburbs, and in fact meetings were often held in the heart of the ghetto where the anguished cries of black people could be heard first hand. Numerous charges of racism in industry, labor organizations, and the public schools were investigated and found to be valid. As a result, new programs and procedures were instituted in many of these agencies. As the commission performed its duties, the residents of the city were made more aware of the problems of racism. Perhaps one of its most important accomplishments was proving that even in a city which has had a long history of Ku Klux Klan activity, change could be made from within the system by the careful and persistent work of a small but committed group of people.[13]

As mentioned in chapter three, some of the most pressing needs for reform in the United

States exist at the *state* level. One Christian who has seriously tried to improve things at this level is Mark Hatfield. As a state legislator he toiled to obtain revision of Oregon's cumbersome constitution and continued his efforts after he became governor. He also undertook a major overhaul of the executive branch of the government to eliminate the overlapping, duplication and inefficiency which was crippling the state administration. He was only partially successful in achieving his goal, but perhaps that is the nature of politics. One seldom accomplishes everything he sets out to do.[14]

At the *national* level the activities of Congressmen Quie and Anderson have already been cited. One area where students in particular were involved in effecting a major change was the Eugene McCarthy presidential campaign in 1968. Thousands of young people enthusiastically pounded the streets and knocked on doors in town after town and state after state to secure votes for their candidate in the various primary elections. Although McCarthy's youthful supporters were bitterly disappointed by the outcome of the Democratic National Convention in Chicago in August of that year, they still played a large part in forcing the retirement of Lyndon Johnson and de-escalating the Vietnam War. Undoubtedly their pressures were felt by Richard Nixon, who finally ended the conflict.

The Potential Christian Impact on Politics/
Individuals can accomplish much by their own willingness to get out and work. On the other hand, there are many things people must do together. In order to achieve maximum effectiveness, large numbers must often band together. This is a fundamental trait of the political process, and Christians should not shy away from it; rather they should lend their full support to political group activity. Sometimes believers will find themselves cooperating with non-Christians. Some did so in joining a popular, interdenominational coalition against the Vietnam War, and perhaps many will take part in a similar association to combat environmental pollution.

On the other hand, there are times when Christians themselves can and should band together to address themselves to some specific issue. After all, this is the point where the political parties often fall short. A party encompasses such a wide range of opinions that its members are frequently unable to agree on how to confront a particular question. Or, its stand on a specific matter is so diluted by compromises reached in order to hold the party together that its position on an issue becomes meaningless. Obviously, a "Christian political party" will not alleviate the situation, but Christians of like mind, working together either within a party or outside the party structure, may be able to achieve something worthwhile on certain problems. The possibilities for evangelical Christians to have a meaningful impact on the present-day political world are almost limitless.

chapter six

Who Will Speak for Martin Niemoeller?

Martin Niemoeller, the courageous German pastor who suffered eight years of imprisonment for his opposition to the Hitler regime, confessed after his release that the German Christian community bore a considerable measure of responsibility for the disaster that had overtaken that unhappy land. "We, that is the Church, have failed, for we knew the wrong and the right path, but we did not warn the people and allowed them to rush forward to their doom."[1] Niemoeller did not exclude himself from this criticism; to the contrary, he acknowledged the fearful results of his own unconcern and noninvolvement in what must be one of the most powerful statements of our time:

> *In Germany they came first for the Communists, and I didn't speak up because I wasn't a Communist. Then they came for the Jews, and I didn't speak up because I wasn't a Jew. Then they came for the trade unionists, and I didn't speak up because I wasn't a trade unionist. Then they came for the Catholics, and I didn't speak up because I was a Protestant. Then they came for me, and by that time no one was left to speak up.*[2]

Thus, Niemoeller becomes a symbol of Christian silence, because, during a period when he as a believer should have taken a stand and spoken out against the Nazi terror, he did not.

The question facing every Christian student today is "Who will speak for Martin Niemoeller?" He and most other German Christians had remained silent about the moral implications of the political drama that had unfolded in their land. Like many believers in the Western democracies currently, the Germans tacitly maintained that they should not "mix religion with politics" but rather should stick to "preaching the gospel" and ministering to the spiritual needs of the people. As the forces of evil spread across the country, the children of God, who had done nothing to resist this development, discovered that they, too, were falling victim to the mounting terror and oppression until finally no one remained to speak up for them.

Today similar forces of evil are on the move in the world. While modern science has made it possible to produce enough to feed, clothe and shelter the entire population of the earth, hundreds of millions still live in grinding poverty. The insane practice of making distinctions between men and subordinating some groups purely on the basis of race or skin color continues unabated. Through modern technology man has created weapons systems that literally can extinguish life from the face of this planet, and the hapless inhabitants of Vietnam have become the victims of the most sophisticated instruments of destruction in the entire history of warfare. What do Christians have to say to these cosmic issues? Will they sit on the sidelines, blissfully indifferent to the great crises of the day? Will they continue to remain silent?

What Do Christian Students Have to Say?/

Fortunately, there are indications that Christian young people are turning against the complacency that now grips and paralyzes a large segment of Western society. In ever-increasing numbers they are rejecting the values of materialism and the lifestyle that emphasizes "getting and having." As Senator Hatfield perceptively noted in one of his recent speeches, "The young of this society feel there must be other motivations than the motivation which is exclusively for profit and dominated by economic consideration. . . . We are looking for a life where people are valued more than things."[3]

A large proportion of the young are also seeking to dismantle the fences and barriers that have kept human beings apart for so long. Many of them are united in the realization that no hope remains for men unless they find some way to work together. Hatfield comments concerning this resurgence of youthful concern, "Even though they may not be approaching the problem through religious convictions, they are coming to know that the world will not function correctly unless man learns to love his fellowman in the same way that God so loved the world that He would not have any man perish."[4]

This statement by the senator from Oregon is particularly noteworthy. That young people "may not be approaching the problem through religious convictions" is a damning indictment of Christianity's failure to provide leadership in this day of deepening crisis. And one cannot brush this fact aside simply by labelling it "secular liberalism and humanism," as many evangelical spokesmen are so accustomed to doing. As we have pointed out, there is indeed a strong biblical basis for the Christian to be working to alleviate the burdens that have fallen upon mankind.

The world belongs to God by right of creation, and he cares for it. He so loved it that he sent his only Son, Jesus Christ, to redeem it and its inhabitants. Christians, those who place their faith in the justifying and redeeming work of God's Son, are ministers in the world. They serve as salt and light to all people on the face of the earth. Because they love their neighbors as themselves, they will see the social imperative of the gospel and become involved in public life in order to insure that the basic human needs of people are met. Genuine Christians minister to the whole man; thus they will not place politics and religion in separate spheres. They are literally the agents of God to bring reconciliation among various individuals, classes, nations and races. Believers are instructed to do good to all men and warned that if their faith is not accompanied by deeds it is dead and of no use. The people of God are expected to exercise stewardship in this world and to serve as a force for good in an environment that on account of sin has become evil and hostile to the Creator.

Of all people, Christian students should recognize and act upon these facts. Christian students are, as we have noted, on the firing line where the issues are and the action is. If younger evangelicals, who are a part of the best informed and most socially aware generation in the twentieth century, do not care, who *will* speak for Martin Niemoeller?

Change and the Christian/

In today's world *change* is the most significant political factor and is likely to remain so for some time. This has tremendous implications for Christian students. Alvin Toffler declared in his bestseller *Future Shock* that "the problem is not, therefore, to suppress change which cannot be done, but to manage it."[5] Yet it is apparent throughout his book that he fails to recognize that man needs a moral basis from which to evaluate changes—in other words, which ones are right and which are wrong? Unfortunately, many believers fear change and, because of this, are seduced into becoming dupes and lackeys of the status quo or, even worse, active agents of reactionary and oppressive movements.

The task before Christian students today is (a) to set their own house in the best possible order and thus earn the right to be heard and (b) to help their elders come to terms with change in a positive manner. Evangelical leader Myron Augsburger stressed at Urbana 70 that the Christian movement desperately needs to free itself from apathy and indifference, refuse to be a part of the status quo and commit itself unreservedly to the lordship of Jesus Christ.

Augsburger further pointed out that Christianity
presently seems to be polarized between "activism" on one side and "pietism" on the other.
This has produced a situation "where the activist
is limited because he can not back up his action
with deep devotional commitment to Christ and
the pietist is limited because he is insecure, in-
effective and irrelevant when it comes to involvement in society." Christians must avoid
both extremes by declaring their commitment to
a higher loyalty or standard, namely, Jesus
Christ.[6]

Thus, as they confront change, Christian
young people have the opportunity to be a positive force for reconciliation within the ranks of
believers. They can unite the pietist and activist
in the common cause by applying biblical perspectives and insights to the rapidly changing
world around them and translating what otherwise might be mere words into positive and
meaningful actions. They can show that in the
Christian outlook on life human values must always take precedence over those of scientism
and technocracy.

At the same time, Christian students can
demonstrate how too much of contemporary
religion has become culture-bound and tied to
materialism, giving sanction to property rights
and selfish gain instead of to more basic human
rights of dignity and freedom. Young people can

revive the revolutionary impulse that lay at the root of early Christianity. The genuinely Christian dimension of concern for the needs of all men can be reasserted as the young escalate their demands for a more just social order. If more believers can be made to understand the full implications of biblical faith, they should be able to adjust to this type of change without going through the trauma of future shock.

The Dangers of Inaction and Wrong Action/

A peril facing evangelical Christians is that they may neglect to bring scriptural values to bear on public affairs because of an unwillingness to participate in civic life. An equally dangerous peril is that Christians may become active on the wrong side of an issue or embrace a cause that is morally wrong from a biblical point of view. For example, moral outrage against the establishment may tempt some evangelical students to join extreme leftist movements, whose main goals call for a renunciation of basic Christian values. Many so-called New Left organizations fall into this category.[7]

On the other hand, Christians can tie themselves too closely to the establishment by embracing doctrinaire political conservatism. Of course, there is no reason why they cannot favor the preservation of the positive aspects of the past without uncritically identifying with the more undesirable institutions and practices of the status quo, but unfortunately this is seldom the case. Sociologists Robert and Helen Lynd assert that such a reactionary posture is all too typical of small-town America where the function of Christianity is "not to raise troublesome questions and to force attention to disparities between values and current practices." [8]

Inaction, identification with some form of materialistic leftist ideology or blind submission to the status quo can all lead to the transformation of Christianity into a culture religion that substitutes itself for a genuine, lively, biblical faith. All political systems and all political ideologies—past, present and future—stand under the transcendent judgment of God, and Christian students should never forget this! [9]

In the meantime, the evils of a culture religion remain a nagging possibility, in some cases a reality, for Christians in Western lands. When it has come into existence, it invariably has been impotent to deal effectively and positively with the problems facing the people in its society. A couple of twentieth-century examples should suffice to underscore the harsh reality of this contention.

The manner in which politics captured Christianity is aptly illustrated by the capitulation of most of Christian Europe to the driving force of nationalism in World War I. In 1914 very few

Christian leaders in Europe publicly and openly condemned the insanity of resolving international differences by armed conflict, and so Christianity was taken prisoner by the fervent nationalism of the time. Who in the Christian community dared to speak out against the carnage? Instead, in every warring country ministers, priests and rabbis blessed the soldiers as they marched off to battle and unceasingly bombarded the Heavenly Father with prayers for victory by *their* armies.

An excellent illustration of this attitude can be found in the memoirs of British Army Chaplain Thomas Tiplady:

Behind the British soldier's thinking stands Christ. Take Christ away, and he would feel as desolate and lost as if you took the sky away. . . . When the soldiers march into the trenches to die for others, they faintly feel that they are following Christ. But they do not speak of it, because they are too humble to compare their self-sacrifice with His.

Well I knew that the lads who had gone over the parapet to their death had seen through the hail of bullets and shells the vision of the crucified Christ welcoming them with outstretched arms. . . . The old world lies in ruins at our feet, and we all build our new and better civilization around the cross.[10]

In the years following World War I, after the

emotionalism of that great conflict had died down, historians began to sort out the issues and separate the rhetoric from the real causes of the war. Whatever the causes—and historians will continue to debate them—it is now clear that all of the participants share responsibility. And it is clear that the leaders of the various powers "used" religion as a part of their national programs to whip up and maintain a high level of support for their respective war efforts. Unfortunately, hindsight is always better than foresight or present-sight. Nevertheless, it is a fearful fact that Christianity was a crucial support in creating and sustaining the ferocity in what was history's greatest war.[11]

The actions of professing Christians in Germany during the years of the Third Reich were little better. It is common knowledge that only a few Lutherans offered meaningful resistance to Nazism, but evangelical scholar David Priestley has shown in a recent study that one of the most orthodox of all the German Christian groups, the Baptists, also loyally supported the regime and even greeted Hitler's accession to power.[12] It is not hard to understand the passiveness of the German Christians once the Third Reich's totalitarian control apparatus had been extended throughout the land, but what had they done before 1933 when Hitler first seized power or before 1936 when he finally consolidated his position? German historian Hannah Vogt has criticized her countrymen, and rightly so, for trying to excuse themselves by saying they did not know about the Nazi crimes nor did they want them to happen. To her fellow Germans she put the penetrating question: "Where were we when we should have opposed the beginnings?" Her response to her own rhetorical statement should be taken seriously by every believing Christian today, regardless of his or her nationality:

> We let the flame of hatred rise and did not extinguish it while there was still time. We allowed posters and songs to spread hatred and abuse while we were still at liberty to fight against them. This first sin of omission gave rise to all the later crimes.[13]

Today's Clarion Call for Political Involvement/
The current situation in the Republic of South Africa and in Rhodesia also points up the problem of Christian inaction and support of the status quo—in this case a degrading apartheid policy. Much the same could be said for the hardline stance of many Protestants in Northern Ireland against full civil rights for the Roman Catholic minority there. And, of course, the record of evangelicals in the United States in blindly supporting the Vietnam War, resisting the movement for racial justice and civil rights,

and objecting to governmental efforts to combat poverty is hardly one of which socially sensitive Christian young people can be proud.

Yet Christians cannot escape their obligation to become involved on the side of justice, truth and humanity in their country's public affairs. In most of the modern democratic states, believers can still participate in politics with a good conscience. To be sure, there are problems in so doing, and we have indicated some of these. But in our contemporary world the opportunities for service presently far outweigh the disadvantages. Christian young people should be encouraged to consider public service as a vocation—one that is every bit as sacred as a calling to the pastoral ministry or foreign missionary service. In support of this point of view Congressman John Anderson has written: "I would like to see some altar calls for men and women who would publicly dedicate themselves to help meet the needs in their home community."[14]

Political involvement is one avenue of expression open to young persons who wish to do something about solving the great problems of our day. The Christian student can pray that God will do something about them; but like the man who prays that the Lord might send out laborers into his harvest (Mt. 9:38), he may discover he has been called to be one of the workers. Further, we have shown that youth possesses the means to exercise a political clout of great significance and that the professional politicians are very much aware of this. Each Christian is called to serve his heavenly Father in some manner, and it is the authors' conviction that many young people will be directed into various forms of public service and political participation. If they are not, only God knows what catastrophes may befall the Western democracies during the final decades of this century!

Forces of evil are abroad in the land and Christians must combat them. There are great issues to be confronted—poverty, racism, war, environmental pollution, drug abuse and many others. Who, in the name of Jesus Christ, will stand and speak for Martin Niemoeller? Will you? *Now is the time to stand, the time to speak!*

Notes

Preface
1/For an example of an issues book by evangelical Christians of a moderate to liberal political persuasion, see Robert G. Clouse, Robert D. Linder and Richard V. Pierard, eds., *The Cross and the Flag* (Carol Stream, Ill.: Creation House, 1972). One with a much more conservative orientation is Kenneth W. Ingwalson, ed., *Your Church—Their Target* (Arlington, Va.: Better Books, 1966).
2/Richard M. Nixon, "Presidential Inaugural Address," *New York Times*, January 21, 1969, p. 21.

Chapter One
1/This information was furnished in confidence by a personal friend of the authors.
2/David O. Moberg, *Inasmuch: Christian Social Re-*

sponsibility in the Twentieth Century (Grand Rapids: Eerdmans, 1965), p. 14.

3/Billy Graham, *Peace with God* (Garden City, N. Y.: Doubleday, 1953), p. 190.

4/Harold Lindsell, ed., *The Church's Worldwide Mission* (Waco, Tex.: Word Books, 1966), p. 235.

5/J. N. D. Anderson, *Into the World: The Need and Limits of Christian Involvement* (London: Falcon Books, 1968), p. 20.

6/Sherwood E. Wirt, *The Social Conscience of the Evangelical* (New York: Harper and Row, 1968), p. 76.

7/Myron Augsburger, in *Christ the Liberator*, John R. W. Stott and others (Downers Grove, Ill.: InterVarsity Press, 1971), pp. 124-25.

8/The definition of politics in this paragraph is the classic Greek one. William Ebenstein, *Great Political Thinkers* (New York: Holt, Rinehart and Winston, 1960), pp. 1-12, 64-75, 209-22, 280. Also see H. F. R. Catherwood, *The Christian Citizen* (London: Hodder and Stoughton, 1969), pp. 32-47.

9/For a fuller, more detailed discussion of evangelical theology based on these foundational statements see the symposium edited by Carl F. H. Henry, *Basic Christian Doctrines* (New York: Holt, Rinehart and Winston, 1962).

10/Ted Ward, *Memo to the Underground* (Carol Stream, Ill.: Creation House, 1971), p. 28.

11/For guidance on this matter see Moberg, *Inasmuch*; Robert D. Linder, "Building Justice in the 70's," *HIS*, 33 (Oct. 1972), 1-3; and the references cited in William M. Pinson, Jr., *Resource Guide to Current Social Issues* (Waco, Tex.: Word Books, 1968).

12/John B. Anderson, *Between Two Worlds: A Congressman's Choice* (Grand Rapids: Zondervan, 1970), p. 149.

Chapter Two

1/Vernon C. Grounds, *Evangelicalism and Social Responsibility* (Scottdale, Pa.: Herald Press, 1969), p. 4.

2/Reprinted in Bruce L. Felknor, *Dirty Politics* (New York: Norton, 1966), p. 128.

3/Alan Kreider, "The Way of Christ," in *Is Revolution Change?*, ed. Brian Griffiths (Downers Grove, Ill.: Inter-Varsity Press, 1972), p. 66.

4/Frederick Catherwood, "Reform or Revolution?" in Ibid., p. 35. The false argument that Christians should avoid political involvement because it is "worldly" can also be applied to holding a job or to any other business activity which necessitates working "in the world." If the spiritual dimension alone is important, why work for mere money forty hours a week?

5/Francis A. Schaeffer, *Pollution and the Death of Man: The Christian View of Ecology* (London: Hodder and Stoughton, 1970), pp. 42-43.

6/Jaymes P. Morgan, Jr., "Why Christian Social Concern?" *Theology, News and Notes,* 11 (Dec. 1967), 4.

7/"Can a Missionary Avoid Politics?" *HIS,* 32 (Nov. 1971), 4-5.

8/Mark O. Hatfield, "How Can a Christian Be in Politics?" in *Protest and Politics: Christianity and Contemporary Affairs,* eds. Robert G. Clouse, Robert D. Linder and Richard V. Pierard (Greenwood, S. C.: Attic Press, 1968), pp. 13-14.

9/Daniel R. Grant, *The Christian and Politics* (Nashville: Broadman Press, 1968), p. 12.

10/Ibid., p. 13.

11/Ralf Dahrendorf, *Society and Democracy in Germany* (New York: Doubleday, 1969), p. 184. See also John H. Bunzel, *Anti-Politics in America* (New York: Knopf, 1967), chapter 1, for a good treatment of the problem of the idealist in politics.

12/A. N. Triton, *Whose World?* (London: Inter-Varsity

Press, 1970), pp. 55, 77.

13/Foy Valentine, *Citizenship for Christians* (Nashville: Broadman Press, 1965), p. 26.

14/Paul G. Elbrecht, *The Christian Encounters Politics and Government* (St. Louis: Concordia Publishing House, 1965), p. 15.

15/George Ladd, "The Christian and the State," *HIS*, 28 (Dec. 1967), 17. See also Oscar Cullmann, *The State in the New Testament* (New York: Scribners, 1956), which is the best work on the topic.

16/Robert G. Clouse displays an obvious anguish as he deals with the alternatives of traditional civil disobedience and revolution in "The Christian, War, and Militarism," in *The Cross and the Flag*, eds., Clouse, Linder and Pierard, pp. 217-36.

17/Ladd, "The Christian and the State," p. 18.

Chapter Three

1/Based on the personal experience of one of the authors.

2/Marcus C. Connally, *The Green Pastures* (New York: Farrar and Rinehart, 1929), p. 69.

3/Mark O. Hatfield, "American Democracy and American Evangelicalism—New Perspectives," *Theology, News and Notes*, 14, No. 4 (Nov. 1970), 9.

4/Cited in Theodore Roszak, *The Making of a Counter Culture* (Garden City, N. Y.: Doubleday, 1968), p. 143.

5/Seymour M. Lipset and Gerald M. Schaflander, *Passion and Politics: Student Activism in America* (Boston: Little, Brown, 1971); Albert H. Cantril and Charles G. Roll, Jr., *The Hopes and Fears of the American People* (New York: Universe Books, 1971).

6/Some other current political questions with moral and spiritual dimensions include separation of church and state, prison reform, population control, drug abuse and crimes of violence.

7/Paul Simon, *The Christian Encounters a Hungry World* (St. Louis: Concordia Publishing House, 1966), p. 61. For another statement of Simon's views on poverty and some practical suggestions as to what to do about it, see his latest book *You Want to Change the World? So Change It!* (New York and Camden: Thomas Nelson, 1971), pp. 72-76.

8/Albert H. Quie, "Church and State in America," in *Congress and Conscience,* ed. John B. Anderson (Philadelphia: Lippincott, 1970), p. 128.

9/Charles E. Goodell and Albert H. Quie, "Poverty in America" and "The Republican Opportunity Crusade As an Alternative to the Anti-Poverty Program," in *Republican Papers,* ed. Melvin R. Laird (Garden City, N. Y.: Doubleday, 1968), pp. 160-90.

10/All of this is recounted in more detail in Anderson, *Between Two Worlds,* chapter 1.

11/Ibid., pp. 4-5.

12/Mark O. Hatfield, *Not Quite So Simple* (New York: Harper and Row, 1968), pp. 154-62.

13/Mark O. Hatfield, "Can a Christian Be a Politician?" *HIS,* 28 (Oct. 1967), 4.

14/Mark O. Hatfield, *Conflict and Conscience* (Waco, Tex.: Word Books, 1971), p. 29.

15/Schaeffer, *Pollution and the Death of Man*; Richard Wright, "Ecology, Magic, and the Death of Man," *Christian Scholar's Review,* 1 (Winter 1971), 117-31; Earl Reeves, "Evangelical Christianity and the Ecological Crisis," in *The Cross and the Flag,* eds., Clouse, Linder and Pierard, pp. 181-201.

16/Interview with Congressman Albert H. Quie, Washington, D. C., January 5, 1973.

17/Cited in Elbrecht, *The Christian Encounters Politics,* p. 57.

18/For example, see Mike Royko, *Boss: Mayor Richard*

J. Daley of Chicago (New York: Dutton, 1971); "Social and Economic Bias Finds Friends at City Hall," *University of Iowa Spectator,* December 1972, p. 6.

19/A Herblock cartoon, copyright 1971.

20/Tom Skinner, *The News in Black and White,* brochure published by Tom Skinner Crusades, Brooklyn, N. Y., 1970, p. 1.

21/John Donne, "Devotions upon Emergent Occasions," XVIII in *The Complete Poetry and Selected Prose of John Donne* (New York: Modern Library, 1941), p. 332.

Chapter Four

1/Jerry Rubin, *Do It!* (New York: Simon and Schuster, 1970), pp. 210, 214-15. Of course, Jerry probably has changed his mind by now.

2/Richard M. Nixon, *It's Time to Stand Up and Be Counted* (Manhattan, Kans.: Kansas State University, 1970), pp. 9, 13.

3/Paul Woodring, *The Higher Learning in America: A Reassessment* (New York: McGraw-Hill, 1968), pp. 68-105, 182-214.

4/Cited in Joseph A. Califano, Jr., *The Student Revolution* (New York: Norton, 1970), p. 90.

5/John Kenneth Galbraith, *The New Industrial State,* rev. ed. (Boston: Houghton, Mifflin, 1971), pp. 283-97, 372-90.

6/Edgar Z. Friedenberg, *The Vanishing Adolescent* (Boston: Beacon Press, 1959), pp. 175-77.

7/The recent Carnegie Commission survey of campus attitudes showed that the political right is present only as a trace whereas the left is distinctly over-represented when compared with the nation as a whole. Moreover, it reported that only 17 percent of the United States public is left-liberal, but 49 percent of all faculty members and 53 percent of all students fall into that category.

8/Califano, *The Student Revolution*, pp. 71-79.

9/Woodring, *The Higher Learning in America*, pp. 57-60; *Chronicle of Higher Education*, 7 (Dec. 18, 1972), 2.

10/Mimeographed text of a speech delivered by Senator Mark O. Hatfield at Bethel College, Kansas, on October 24, 1971, p. 9.

11/This observation is based upon the personal experiences of the authors as campaign workers, managers and candidates in local elections.

12/Roy Hoopes, *Getting With Politics* (New York: Dell, 1968), p. 88.

13/Cited in Wirt, *The Social Conscience of the Evangelical*, p. 91.

Chapter Five

1/Walfred H. Peterson, "The Responsibility of the Christian Voter," in *Protest and Politics*, eds., Clouse, Linder and Pierard, pp. 32-33.

2/Ibid., pp. 26-29. For another sound discussion of this same subject, see Ronald Michaelson, "Positive Politics," *HIS*, 32 (May 1972), 11-13.

3/Hoopes, *Getting With Politics*, p. 130.

4/Ibid., pp. 132-33.

5/Catherwood, *The Christian Citizen*, pp. 173-74.

6/Francis A. Schaeffer, *The Church at the End of the 20th Century* (Downers Grove, Ill.: InterVarsity Press, 1970), p. 133.

7/Peterson, "The Responsibility of the Christian Voter," pp. 25-26.

8/William M. Pinson, Jr., "Why All Christians Are Called into Politics," in *Politics: A Guidebook for Christians*, ed. James M. Dunn (Dallas: Christian Life Commission, Baptist General Convention of Texas, 1970), pp. 19-20.

9/"Who Should Run Your Town? Maybe You," *Changing Times*, 25 (Nov. 1971), 40.

10/Earle E. Cairns, *Saints and Society* (Chicago: Moody Press, 1960), p. 111. The biographical sketches are taken from chapter 3 of this book.

11/Kathleen Heasman, *Evangelicals in Action* (London: Geoffrey Bles, 1962).

12/Foy Valentine, "How to Preach on Political Issues," *The Baptist Program*, March 1972, p. 11.

13/Letter in the authors' files.

14/Hatfield, *Not Quite So Simple*, chapter 4.

Chapter Six

1/Martin Niemoeller, "About the Question of Guilt," *Christianity and Crisis*, 6 (July 8, 1946), 1.

2/Quotation contained in a recent undated brochure issued by the Institute for American Democracy, Washington, D. C.

3/Mimeographed text of a speech delivered at Bethel College, Kansas, on October 24, 1971, p. 4.

4/Mark O. Hatfield, "Introduction," in Anderson, *Between Two Worlds*, p. ix.

5/Alvin Toffler, *Future Shock* (New York: Bantam Books, 1971), p. 379.

6/Augsburger, in *Christ the Liberator*, pp. 123, 128.

7/Paul B. Henry, "Evangelical Christianity and the Radical Left," in *The Cross and the Flag*, eds. Clouse, Linder and Pierard, pp. 81-98.

8/Robert S. Lynd and Helen Merrill Lynd, *Middletown in Transition* (New York: Harcourt, Brace, 1937), p. 316.

9/Paul B. Henry, "The Politics of Religion," *Reformed Journal*, 22 (Dec. 1972), 7-8.

10/Thomas Tiplady, *The Cross at the Front* (New York: Fleming H. Revell, 1917), pp. 74-75, 114-15.

11/For insight into these matters, see Sidney Fay's classic study *The Origins of the World War*, rev. ed., 2 vols. (New York: Macmillan, 1966): Laurence Lafore, *The Long Fuse* (Philadelphia: Lippincott, 1965); Erich Maria Remarque, *All Quiet on the Western Front* (Boston: Little, Brown, 1929); and Arnold Zweig, *Education Before Verdun* (New York: Viking Press, 1936).

12/David T. Priestley, "The Baptist Response in Germany to the Third Reich," in *God and Caesar: Case Studies in the Relationship Between Christianity and the State*, ed. Robert D. Linder (Longview, Tex.: Conference on Faith and History, 1971), pp. 102-23.

13/Hannah Vogt, *The Burden of Guilt* (New York: Oxford Univ. Press, 1964), p. 234. See Richard V. Pierard, "The Golden Image of Nebuchadnezzar," *Reformed Journal*, 22 (Dec. 1972), 9-13.

14/Anderson, *Between Two Worlds*, p. 150.

For Further Study

An asterisk (*) denotes those books available in paperback.

Anderson, J. N. D. **Into the World: The Need and Limits of Christian Involvement.** *London: Falcon Books, 1968.* *
A British evangelical stresses the need for Christians to be wholeheartedly involved in the life of the contemporary world.

Anderson, John B. **Between Two Worlds: A Congressman's Choice.** *Grand Rapids: Zondervan, 1970.* *
A book about political institutions and ideas from the point of view of a Christian congress-

man. Especially helpful in showing how a Christian conscience can sometimes change one's political outlook over the course of time.

Anderson, John B., ed. **Congress and Conscience.** *Philadelphia: Lippincott, 1970.*
A collection of six essays by members of Congress who are also active churchmen. Especially valuable are the contributions of Congressmen Jim Wright on "Legislation and the Will of God," John Anderson on "American Protestantism and Political Ideology" and Senator George S. McGovern on "The Politics of Hunger."

Catherwood, H. F. R. **The Christian in Industrial Society.** *London: Tyndale Press, 1964.**
An excellent and sometimes heady discussion of the Christian attitude toward political and economic institutions in the modern world. Included as an appendix is an enlightened examination of the Weber-Tawney thesis.

———. **The Christian Citizen.** *London: Hodder and Stoughton, 1969.**
A prominent English evangelical who is himself "involved" makes a strong case for the participation of Christians in solving the social and political problems of the world today.

Clouse, Robert G., Robert D. Linder, and Richard V. Pierard, eds. **The Cross and the Flag.** *Carol Stream, Ill.: Creation House, 1972.**

Eleven scholars discuss a broad range of important current issues from an evangelical Christian point of view.

————. **Protest and Politics: Christianity and Contemporary Affairs.** *Greenwood, S. C.: Attic Press, 1968.*
A symposium on contemporary problems and their relationship to Christian concerns.

Cullmann, Oscar. **The State in the New Testament.** *New York: Scribners, 1956.* *
The best book on the subject in English by one of the outstanding twentieth-century authorities on the New Testament and early Christian history.

De Koster, Lester. **Communism and the Christian Faith.** *Grand Rapids: Eerdmans, 1962.*
The most important book on communism by an evangelical Christian in recent years. It endeavors to show what communists really believe and how this is related to basic Christian ideas.

Elbrecht, Paul G. **The Christian Encounters Politics and Government.** *St. Louis and London: Concordia, 1965.* *
A work which calls Christians to the opportunities for service within the American political system. Written by an evangelical who has been there.

Furness, Charles. **The Christian and Social Action.** *Westwood, N. J.: Fleming H. Revell, 1972.*

A faculty member of a prominent evangelical Bible college intelligently discusses the biblical basis for Christian social concern and activity.

Grant, Daniel R. **The Christian and Politics.** *Nashville: Broadman Press, 1968.* *
A good practical introduction to the subject by a Christian political scientist and educator.

Griffiths, Brian. **Is Revolution Change?** *Downers Grove, Ill., and London: InterVarsity Press, 1972.* *
Five essays by evangelicals who stress that Christians should play a major role in working for social and political reform in order to render violent revolutions unnecessary.

Grounds, Vernon C. **Revolution and the Christian Faith.** *Philadelphia: Lippincott, 1971.* *
A sensitive, in-depth examination of the concept of revolution, presented from a distinctly Christian perspective.

Hatfield, Mark O. **Conflict and Conscience.** *Waco, Tex.: Word Books, 1971.*
A splendid example of how one of the best-known evangelical Christian statesmen of our time relates his personal faith in Christ to his involvement in politics. In this book, Senator Hatfield explains how his humanitarian political outlook grows out of his Christian commitment.

———. **Not Quite So Simple.** *New York: Harper*

and Row, 1968.
The political autobiography of a Christian who has served in a variety of high elective political offices. He cogently presents the "how" and "why" of his career in politics.

Henry, Carl F. H. **A Plea for Evangelical Demonstration.** *Grand Rapids: Baker, 1971.*
Building upon his earlier, highly-regarded works on Christian social ethics, this noted evangelical theologian issues a call for involvement in societal problems.

Linder, Robert D., ed. **God and Caesar: Case Studies in the Relationship between Christianity and the State.** *Longview, Tex.: The Conference on Faith and History, 1971.* *
In this collection of essays, evangelicals from several different denominations analyze the historic difficulties encountered by Christians in various lands as they struggled to relate biblical faith to the demands of the state.

Maston, T. B. **The Christian, The Church, and Contemporary Problems.** *Waco, Tex.: Word Books, 1968.*
A significant discussion of current problems by a well-known Southern Baptist author and professor.

Moberg, David O. **The Great Reversal: Evangelism Versus Social Concern.** *Philadelphia: Lip-*

pincott, 1972.
A treatment of two important questions: Why did evangelical Christianity, the leader in social welfare and reform prior to the twentieth century, discontinue its active role in this, and is a commitment to personal evangelism compatible with an interest in social issues and politics?

————. **Inasmuch: Christian Social Responsibility in the 20th Century.** *Grand Rapids: Eerdmans, 1965.* *
A Christian sociologist's forthright plea for evangelical social action, particularly stressing the biblical backgrounds for it. Contains a great number of practical helps.

Niebuhr, Reinhold. **The Children of Light and the Children of Darkness.** *New York: Scribners, 1944.* *
One of America's ablest neo-orthodox theologians gives a first-rate treatment of the relationship of Christianity and politics.

Pierard, Richard V. **The Unequal Yoke: Evangelical Christianity and Political Conservatism.** *Philadelphia: Lippincott, 1970.* *
A re-examination of the current alliance in America between orthodox Christendom and the status quo.

Rutenber, Culbert G. **The Dagger and the Cross.** *Nyack, N. Y.: Fellowship Publications, 1958.* *
A well-known Baptist leader expounds Christian

pacifism and its biblical foundations.

Salley, Columbus and Ronald Behm. **Your God Is Too White.** *Downers Grove, Ill.: InterVarsity Press, 1970.* *
Every Christian should read this book on Christianity and racism. If it does not provoke evangelicals to thought, discussion and action in this area of concern, then probably nothing will.

Schaeffer, Francis A. **Pollution and the Death of Man: The Christian View of Ecology.** *Wheaton, Ill.: Tyndale House; London: Hodder and Stoughton, 1970.* *
In this brief volume, a leading evangelical Christian spokesman discusses one of the most important issues of our day. A good place to start.

――――. **The Church at the End of the 20th Century.** *Downers Grove, Ill.: InterVarsity Press; London: Norfolk Press, 1970.* *
An important book analyzing the relationship between the contemporary Christian church and culture. It includes a discussion of the New Left, the establishment, ecology, social engineering and the need for individual and institutional reform in order to meet the needs of mankind in the last three decades of the twentieth century.

Simon, Paul. **You Want to Change the World? So Change It!** *New York and Camden: Thomas Nelson, 1971.* *
The former lieutenant governor of Illinois, a

dedicated Lutheran layman, argues persuasively that young people can bring about change and offers sane, practical advice on how to grapple with specific political and social problems.

Spitzer, Walter O. and Carlyle L. Saylor, eds. **Birth Control and the Christian: A Symposium by the Christian Medical Society and Christianity Today.** *Wheaton, Ill.: Tyndale House; London: Coverdale, 1969.*
A collection of papers by Christian scholars dealing with the ethical and theological problems surrounding the control of human reproduction. A pioneer work in its field.

Streiker, Lowell D. and Gerald S. Strober. **Religion and the New Majority: Billy Graham, Middle America and the Politics of the 70s.** *New York: Association Press, 1972.*
A fascinating analysis of what the authors believe is an emerging new political majority in America symbolized by the warm friendship of President Richard Nixon and evangelist Billy Graham. Most evangelicals will view their conclusions with mixed feelings of horror and delight.

Valentine, Foy. **The Cross and the Marketplace.** *Waco, Tex.: Word Books, 1966.*
A solid little work offering Christian perspectives on racism, communism, political morality and Christian social action.

Ward, Ted. **Memo to the Underground.** *Carol Stream, Ill.: Creation House, 1971.*
Directed at the younger generation, this provocative, pithy work encourages student involvement in both church renewal and social action.

Wirt, Sherwood E. **The Social Conscience of the Evangelical.** *New York: Harper and Row; London: Scripture Union, 1968.*
A prominent evangelical journalist urges his fellow believers to come to grips with many of the pressing issues of the day. A good beginning on many current political problems and social issues.

Yoder, John Howard. **The Politics of Jesus.** *Grand Rapids: Eerdmans, 1972.* *
The dean of Mennonite scholars shows that the teachings and ministry of Jesus reveal a coherent and relevant approach to the fundamental issues of Christian activity in the world.

Index

Robert D. Linder *is professor of history at Kansas State University, Manhattan. He earned the Ph.D. in history at the University of Iowa and has been at KSU since 1965. His specialties are the Reformation, and the history of religious and political ideas and movements. He is the author of* The Political Ideas of Pierre Viret *(1964) and co-author of* Protest and Politics: Christianity and Contemporary Affairs *(1968),* Calvin and Calvinism: Sources of Democracy? *(1970),* God and Caesar: Case Studies in the Relationship Between Christianity and the State *(1971) and* The Cross and the Flag *(1972). He also is editor of* Fides et Historia, *the journal of the Conference on Faith and History. Linder was elected to the Manhattan City Commission in 1969 and served as mayor of the city in 1971-72. At KSU he received the outstanding teacher award in 1968 and is the IVCF chapter's faculty sponsor. He is a member of the Republican Party and an active Baptist churchman.*

Richard V. Pierard *is professor of history at Indiana State University, Terre Haute. He received the Ph.D. in history at the University of Iowa and joined the ISU faculty in 1964. His areas of interest are modern Germany, nineteenth- and twentieth-century European overseas expansion, and contemporary conservative movements and ideologies. He is author of* The Unequal Yoke: Evangelical Christianity and Political Conservatism *(1970), and co-author of* Protest and Politics *(1968) and* The Cross and the Flag *(1972). He is secretary-treasurer of the Conference on Faith and History, and in 1971 spent a sabbatical leave serving as a guest lecturer at the Greater Europe Mission's Bibelschule Bergstrasse in Germany. In the May, 1972, primary election, Pierard was a candidate for delegate to the Indiana State Democratic Party Convention. He works closely with the ISU chapter of IVCF and is a member of the Terre Haute Christian Reformed Church.*